Simple Habits for Marital Happiness

Simple Habits for Marital Happiness

Randall Schroeder, Ph.D.

CrossLink Publishing

CrossLink Publishing
1601 Mt. Rushmore Rd, STE 3288
Rapid City, SD 57702

Ordering Information:
Quantity sales. Special discounts are available on quantity purchases by corporations, associations, and others. For details, contact the "Special Sales Department" at the address above.

Simple Habits for Marital Happiness/Schroeder —1st ed.

ISBN 978-1-63357-175-4

Library of Congress Control Number: 2019943060

First edition: 10 9 8 7 6 5 4 3 2 1

Front Cover Design: Brent A Cooper - Cooper Creations Graphic Design

WHAT OTHERS ARE SAYING

"*Simple Habits for Marital Happiness* is a great guidebook for anyone genuinely wanting to understand the heart of their spouse. Dr. Schroeder has done a wonderful job giving practical insight on how to make immediate and lasting improvements in any marriage. You'll keep going back to this book over and over." **Stephen Arterburn**, New York Times Best Selling author of books such as *Every Man's Battle*, editor of the *Life Recovery Bible,* Founder of New Life Ministries and host of New Life Live, creator of Women of Faith conferences, and Teaching Pastor Northview Church, Carmel, Indiana

"After more than 50 years of marriage, one would think that my dear wife and I have each other figured out well enough to be able to avoid disagreements and to keep stressful moments from becoming harmful conversations or hurtful actions. Think again. We still have our share of misunderstandings and hurt feelings. Dr. Schroeder's practical recommendations in **Simple Habits for Marital Happiness** will help married couples achieve greater understanding, emotional attachment, mutual happiness, and spiritual unity. It would be a great gift idea for married friends, children, and grandchildren." **Rev. Dr. Gerald Kieschnick**, President Emeritus of The Lutheran Church-Missouri Synod and Chief Executive Officer of Legacy Deo

"Dr. Schroeder has given a wealth of practical wisdom and insight into developing and maintaining a healthy marital relationship. His beginning with forgiveness and the power it gives for reconciliation is excellent and sets this book apart from many other practical marital guides. His 4 wisdom habits are simple, yet profound: eye contact, hugs, kisses, and time together. I see the necessary ingredient in communication with his constant emphasis on affirmation and respect. This book will be an excellent guide for spiritual closeness that can benefit a couple for their lifetime." **Rev. Dr. David Ludwig** author of *Renewing the Family Spirit, The Spirit of Your Marriage, The Power of WE*, and *Christian Concepts for Care*

"What a gem of a book for anyone who wants their marriage to grow stronger, healthier and more loving – which is just about everyone I know! Chock full of practical, easy-to-read tips that deal with real-life marital issues—from 'date your mate' to handling your finances—Dr. Schroeder's book is a must-have daily reader that will keep you coming back for more!" **Michele Chynoweth**, author of contemporary, bible-based novels *The Faithful One, The Peace Maker, The Runaway Prophet* and *The Jealous Son*

"Drawing upon nearly three decades as an effective Christian therapist and marriage counselor, Dr. Schroeder brings together a valuable collection of lessons aimed at bolstering marital relationships. The tenuousness of the marriage bond is reflected in the sad statistic of so many marital failures—a result that no couple beginning lives together anticipates or desires. Habits and behaviors that contribute to a successful marriage are not simply intuitive. This volume, comprised of 90 short, very practical topics, offers help, guidance, and encouragement based on a solid Biblical foundation, committed Christian faith, and keen insight from therapy research and practice. *Simple Habits for Marital Happiness* is a fine resource and wonderful blessing for any couple eager to enjoy a happy marriage." **Rev. Dr. Patrick Ferry**, President, Concordia University Wisconsin

"As a parish pastor, I was always looking for resources to share with married couples. Dr. Schroeder has put together an outstanding resource for helping couples improve their communication and strengthen their marriages. I believe **Simple Habits for Marital Happiness** will be an excellent tool for pastors in their marital and premarital counseling. It is a tool they will be able to use almost immediately in helping couples build healthier and stronger marriages." **Rev. Dr. Steven Turner**, President of the Iowa West LCMS District

"**Simple Habits for Marital Happiness** is practical, Pastoral and grounded in helpful Biblical wisdom for today's challenged marriages. These habits offer hope! These habits remind us that God intends marriages to be relationships of Joy through Christ. Dr. Schroeder (one of my Seminary Professors) is not a travel agent 'who has never been where he wants us to go' but a tour guide 'who has been there and who has walked with couples' to improve lives and marriages. I loved the examples and his many years of experience with thousands of couples and individuals come through. This is an intriguing read and it applies to life and marriages in the most basic ways." **Rev. Dr. Allan Buss**, President of the Northern Illinois LCMS District

"Dr. Schroeder has offered to married couples (or those contemplating marriage) an excellent and timely tool. At a time when marriages are crumbling at an all-time rate, his **Simple Habits for Marital Happiness** is not only a 'how to' but also a 'who to' resource. Drawing from his experience as a long time Individual, Family, and Marriage counselor he presents practical and attainable habits for the couple, but also stresses that those efforts must reflect a partnership between a man and a woman who understand 'who to' rely upon for their inspiration to succeed. The habits are not only a recovery strategy, but a foundation for a healthier marriage for us all. Thank you, Dr. Schroeder, for helping us make healthier marriages a habit for our lives together." **Rev. Keith Kohlmeier**, Former President of the Kansas LCMS District

WHAT HAPPY COUPLES ARE SAYING

"We wanted to tell you that you are the best thing that ever happened to us and you saved our marriage with the simple habits."

"Simple habits saved us from the brink of divorce. After 30 years of marriage, we had lost our connection with one another and as a result of the simple habits we found increased closeness and bonding, we reconnected and we became best friends again."

"Our marriage started to improve immediately when we learned how to properly request expectations (a simple habit) rather than just guess at what was expected."

"The simple habits did more than emotionally connect us as a couple, we were individually strengthened as spouses and drawn together in unity as we worked together for the common goal of marital satisfaction."

"Thank you for your outstanding leadership in guiding us from conflict to a more satisfying marriage with the simple habits."

"Thank you for helping us save our marriage and family! Without your help with the simple habits, our little angel would have never been born."

"We knew date your mate was important but simply understanding 'how to' have dates made a significant difference in our happiness."

"Words cannot express the gratitude I feel in my heart! You have helped us through a troubled time to have the gift of a good marriage turned to terrific."

"We both very much appreciate your expertise and knowledge in helping our marriage with the simple habits."

"We have come a long way this year in our personal lives and marriage, and are grateful for your guidance with the simple habits."

My spouse and I are both very grateful for your time, your simple habits, and your special way of helping us through a rough time in our marriage."

"You have helped enrich our marriage with the simple habits."

"Thank you for all that you have done to help us become happier and healthier in our marriage."

I dedicate this book to the glory of God!

Words cannot express my sincere gratitude for my wonderful wife, Ginny, who has been the love of my life for over forty years. Her unwavering belief in me to write a book that will benefit thousands of marriages was an endless encouragement.

I am also deeply thankful for the steadfast, loving support from our sons, daughters-in-law, and grandchildren.

Contents

ACKNOWLEDGMENTS

I am deeply indebted to numerous couples who made this book a reality. They allowed me to understand the intimate details of their lives and marriage in order to help them create a satisfying relationship. I sincerely appreciate their willingness to change and improve their marriages through the implementation of the *Simple Habits* found in these lessons.

INTRODUCTION

No one ever ties the knot expecting to get divorced. Everyone who gets married wants their marriage to be satisfying and rewarding. Unfortunately, a majority of spouses are disappointed in their relationship, and sadly, that results in a high divorce rate and an even greater percentage of unhappy marriages. Many couples suffer needlessly because spouses simply do not possess the practical wisdom and simple skills for achieving the goal of a happy marriage. No one ever taught them how, and they might not have had good role models in their own household growing up.

A desire for a satisfying relationship is what propels a marriage in a positive direction. However, the desire alone is not enough. A healthy, happy marriage is built—or a marriage in trouble crumbles—day by day through the specific, small actions that show our love or disdain for our spouse. The good news is that anyone can learn to develop the habits that create a gratifying marriage!

The Bible encourages, "Correct your **habits** and **change your actions for the better**" (Jeremiah 18:11 AMP). The central theme for happy couples can be summarized in three words— HEALTHY, GODLY HABITS! *Simple Habits for Marital Happiness* is designed to immediately improve your marriage and transform your relationship into daily satisfaction. Each lesson can be read in less than five minutes and is intended to strengthen your present positive behaviors or help repair troubling parts of your relationship.

Simple Habits for Marital Happiness is different from other Christian marriage books because it is filled with relationship wisdom in short, easily achievable lessons. The book is divided into seven chapters to strengthen every aspect of your marriage. *Simple Habits for Marital Happiness* does not speak in undefined ideas, but instead has very precise, helpful advice for real-world situations. In doing so, it also diffuses the most common arguments going on in households across the country.

Proverbs 4:5 speaks to every spouse seeking a satisfying marriage: "Get [skillful and godly] wisdom! Acquire understanding" (AMP). Godly wisdom and skills are the goals found throughout *Simple Habits for Marital Happiness*. With this book, you have all the practical answers necessary for achieving a gratifying marriage. And the implementation of just one healthier habit often makes the difference between marital happiness and divorce.

Simple Habits for Marital Happiness can either be read as a step-by-step program or a do-it-yourself fix-it manual. Most spouses will begin with chapter 1 because forgiveness is the foundation for spiritual, emotional, and relational oneness. However, if your marriage is seriously hurting, you might initially read another lesson that addresses a particular concern.

This how-to book will provide practical behaviors and helpful ideas for spouses wanting to strengthen their marriage, couples struggling in troubled relationships, and newlyweds wanting to learn healthy behaviors to establish a lifelong, satisfying marriage.

CHAPTER I

THE HABIT AT THE HEART OF YOUR CHRISTIAN MARRIAGE: *FORGIVENESS*

Adam and Eve sinned and placed a wall between all mankind and God. Forgiveness of sins was the only way to break down the barrier between God and mankind. Again and again, the essential importance of forgiveness is mentioned throughout the Old and New Testaments. The entire substance of the Christian faith is forgiveness. Hence, Christianity may appropriately be called the **good news of forgiveness**.

Just as forgiveness is at the center of Christianity, forgiveness is at the heart of a happy marriage. The Bible has nearly 125 references to the importance of forgiveness for interpersonal relationships. The entire substance of the Christian faith is forgiveness, and likewise the "glue" for every marriage is apologizing and forgiving. A satisfying marriage contains two spouses with humility and courage because it is humbling to apologize and takes courage to forgive. Hurts or sins occur within every Christian marriage. When spouses have the momentous goal to apologize and forgive one another for marital hurts or sins, these two actions will significantly increase the probabilities for a gratifying Christian relationship.

No marriage is perfect because married life is a combination of Christlike actions coupled with sinful words and behaviors.

Like all couples, you will not always have ideal communication, agreeably resolve all your disagreements, and be on the same emotional wavelength. At times, heartache and heartburn happen within every healthy relationship. Whenever you experience a hurt or disappointment, you probably have some degree of resentment or ill will. Over time, such bitterness can build an emotional wall in your marriage. The only avenue for resolving any marital frustration is forgiveness.

One of the main contributors to divorce is an absence of willingness to apologize to one another and forgive each other. The apostle Paul encourages every spouse: "Be kind and helpful to one another, tender-hearted [compassionate, understanding], forgiving one another [readily and freely], just as God in Christ also forgave you" (Ephesians 4:32 AMP). Hence, this chapter focuses not only on specific godly behaviors, but it also provides an essential understanding of the apologizing and forgiving process. Without forgiveness, it is almost impossible to have a satisfying long-term relationship.

1. UNDERSTAND WHY FORGIVENESS IS THE "GLUE"

On a human level, the central tenet of the Christian faith is interpersonal restoration through forgiveness. Jesus said, "But if you refuse to forgive others, your Father will not forgive your sins" (Matthew 6:15 NLT). Even while being crucified on a cross, Jesus said, "Father, forgive them" (Luke 23:34 NIV). *Forgiveness* is always beneficial because it alone can repair relationships—with God, others, and your spouse. Forgiveness is a lifelong essential ingredient for maintaining a gratifying marriage. Forgiveness of sins is truly the greatest blessing for every couple.

If a marriage is broken, only forgiveness can *glue* the relationship back together. Without forgiveness, you and your spouse will build an ever-growing wall between the two of you. I use three analogies to help couples understand the damage done by unforgiven wrongs, as well as the benefits associated with healing those wounds.

First, think of marital harmony like a lush fairway on a golf course. *Apologizing* and *forgiving* is like replacing a divot after a golf shot in the fairway. While playing golf, whenever a divot is made, the polite action is to either replace the divot or place sand with grass seed in the divot. If divots are not repaired, the golf course will turn into all dirt and no one will want to play on that course. However, when divots are repaired, the golf course remains green and lush and is an attractive place to enjoy friendship and God's creation.

Likewise, just dealing with day-to-day life issues, every so often, *marital divots* will unfortunately occur. When you do not replace your divots by apologizing and forgiving, the likelihood of a satisfying marriage is diminished because your "marriage golf course" will become more and more barren.

For a second analogy, think about what it would be like to try to wallpaper a room that's filled with steam—certainly an impossible task. You can try to wallpaper that room until Jesus returns, but the walls will be so damp and moist that the wallpaper will never stick and it will keep sliding down. You will need to open the door and let the steam out of the room, so the walls can dry. Then, you can beautify the room with wallpaper.

Similarly, if your heart or your spouse's heart is filled with the steam of bitterness and resentment, you can demonstrate all the nice actions in the world, but you will be unable to beautify your marital hearts because of the negative steam. Apologizing and forgiving one another allows the steam of bitterness to leave your heart. Healthy words and actions now have the opportunity to beautify your relationship once again.

Let's look at the third example. Let's say that tonight you have spaghetti for supper and you do not wash your plates but instead set them on the kitchen counter. Tomorrow night, you have barbecued chicken. You eat off those same two dirty plates and once again do not wash them. Then, the next night you eat chicken fried steak with cream gravy on those dirty plates, and once again you do not wash them and return the plates to the kitchen counter. By repeatedly eating off dirty plates, eventually with the bacteria buildup, you will contract food poisoning.

A poisoned relationship is what happens when unforgiven wrongs exist in your marriage. Relational bruises and emotional injuries will create "dirty plates." Yet, apologizing and forgiving washes your dirty plates to prevent the poisoning. By eating off clean plates each day, you take no chances with hurting your relationship.

If your marriage has numerous unrepaired divots, hearts filled with the steam of resentment, and dirty plates, your relationship will probably be stressed and tense. I hope these mental pictures will help you understand why apologizing and forgiving are the *glue* for every healthy relationship. Definitely, *apologizing and forgiving* are always the first steps in restoring a broken marriage.

2. REPENTANCE, NOT JUST REGRET

Only *repentance* will benefit your marriage, *never just regret*. I define regret as merely a whimsical wish, but not a strong commitment for changing unhealthy words or behaviors. Regret is basically more of a feeling or just verbal expression of a hopeful change. Examples of regret are: "I wish I would stop being unfaithful"; "I wish I could stop calling my spouse names"; "I wish I would control my compulsive spending habits"; "I wish I would cease my controlling ways"; etc. Simply, *regret is a meaningless repent* because the offense is going to be repeated. If either of you believe regret is sufficient, that will be poisonous for your marriage.

On the other hand, *repentance* is a strong desire for a behavioral improvement, an absolute 180-degree turnaround in a positive direction for a godly change of action and attitude. In Ezekiel

18, God tells us to "repent and live." Likewise, a marriage will not have life without repentance. *Repentance* is a clear commitment to never again demonstrate the unhealthy words or behaviors that damaged your relationship. Without repentance, it is almost impossible to restore your relationship because only through continual improvements with wholesome words and behaviors can you have a rewarding relationship.

Repentance is comprised of three parts: *emotional*, *mental*, and *behavioral*. *Emotionally*, the offending spouse feels remorse, sorrow, and sadness resulting from the pain caused by their wound. Repentance is simply heartfelt sorrow for a marital injury. *Mentally*, an offending spouse makes a cognitive decision, a sincere change of mind, to never commit that wrong again. Although repentance begins in the heart, it is a mental decision to return once again to godly living. *Behaviorally*, with God's help the offending spouse makes an honest effort to never do that wrong another time. So, a repentant spouse has such sorrow that there is a new determination with a promise to never allow that marital wound to ever happen again.

An example of regret is a wife I counseled who had experienced physical abuse for years from her husband. Often in abusive relationships, the mistreatment escalates over the years from verbal and emotional abuse to physical abuse. In her initial appointment, she reported physical injuries that placed her in the emergency room. Similar to previous abusive episodes, her husband expressed regret over his actions and even told her, "I hope you do not upset me again because I don't want to hit you." Yes, like too many abusers, he did not accept responsibility for his damaging actions.

I encouraged the wife to forgive her husband but not return home until she was confident that he was absolutely repentant and not just regretful. She agreed with me on forgiving him but did not agree with my idea of confirming his repentance. In less than a month, he sent her to the emergency room, but this time the injuries were so severe she spent several days in the hospital.

Again, I stressed the importance of forgiving her husband. I also pleaded with her to take their children and live with her parents until she was absolutely confident that her husband would seek professional help. I never mentioned the word *divorce* but only stressed safety for her and their children. I advised that unless he learned cognitive and behavioral coping skills for effectively handling his damaging words and behaviors, further verbal and physical abuse would not only occur, but probably escalate. She not only did not agree with me but went back home with her husband and ceased to attend future counseling sessions. I never heard if her injuries continued, but I pray that she learned the difference between regret and repentance. Understanding the importance of repentance is absolutely essential with abuse because harmful words and behaviors are never condoned by God or a healthy spouse.

In addition, understand there is a window of time associated with *repentance* versus *regret*. In other words, there needs to be a period of time where the offense is not committed again. For example, if you call your spouse a harmful name today, then in a positive manner immediately apologize, seek forgiveness, and your spouse forgives you, such wholesome apologizing and forgiving would normally restore your marital connection. However, if tomorrow and nearly every day thereafter, you continue calling your spouse toxic names—that is only regret. Even if you apologize and seek forgiveness, such ongoing horrible name-calling really defines regretful behavior and not genuine repentance.

On the other hand, when you are *repentant*, there is a lengthy space of time between offenses. Perhaps both of you will define that window of time differently. Hence, if you call your spouse a harmful name today, then repent, apologize, seek forgiveness, and are forgiven by your spouse, hopefully at a minimum, that toxic name-calling will not occur for several months or even longer. However, with serious offenses like adultery or physical abuse, there is no window of time because an absolute change of ways must occur so that those destructive behaviors NEVER happen again for your entire marriage.

Repentance, a change of ways in a godly direction, is what leads to restoration of your relationship. Without genuine repentance for every marital offense, a relationship will probably never be satisfying. A significant goal for each of you is a strong desire for repentance for your harmful words and behaviors.

3. UNDERSTAND WHY FORGIVENESS IS SO DIFFICULT

Forgiveness is extremely difficult for all of us. Forgiveness required atonement for sin, the sacrifice of God's only Son, Jesus Christ. John 3:16 states, "For God so loved the world that he gave his one and only Son, that whoever believes in him shall not perish but have eternal life" (NIV). Our heavenly Father lovingly sent His only begotten Son to pay the price for the sins of the world on that rugged cross. If forgiveness required the ultimate sacrifice from God, His only Son, will forgiveness ever be an easy step for you?

No one is born with the talent of forgiveness because, sadly, an unforgiving spirit is actually part of our humanity. Hence, almost every spouse needs pragmatic direction on how to apologize and forgive. And acquiring the skill of forgiveness can only be learned through repetition. Since forgiveness is an unknown competency and unquestionably the most difficult action in the universe, it is no wonder that most marriages lack apologizing and forgiving skills. So why do we battle with the most significant component for a rich, rewarding marriage? Due to a number of reasons, *apologizing and forgiving* are significant challenges for most spouses.

Pride is usually at the inner fight with possessing a forgiving spirit. Proverbs 11:2 states, "When pride comes [boiling up with an arrogant attitude of self-importance], then come dishonor and shame, but with the humble [the teachable who have been chiseled by trial and who have learned to walk humbly with God] there is wisdom and soundness of mind" (AMP). "Knowledge makes people arrogant, but love builds them up" (1 Corinthians 8:1 GW). I believe that a prideful spirit is at the core of all sins. The sin of pride is an inward focus on self and a refusal to submit to God's ways. Proverbs 13:10 declares, "Where there is strife, there is pride, but wisdom is found in those who take advice" (NIV). Pride produces disharmony as Romans 12:16 declares, "Live in harmony with one another. Do not be proud, but be willing to associate with people of low position. Do not be conceited" (NIV).

When pride makes apologizing difficult, a spouse has a superior attitude, and that self-righteousness blocks both an apologizing and forgiving spirit. Thus, a prideful spouse does not view the other partner as equal, and rarely if ever, does a prideful spouse believe their partner deserves an apology or forgiveness. Pride often is manipulative, as even the thoughts behind a forgiving spirit could be motivated by self-centeredness. Proverbs 16:18 warns, "Pride goes before destruction, and a haughty spirit before a fall" (AMP), and that "fall" is many times into the abyss of unhappiness or even divorce.

Like most beliefs and behaviors, example is both the greatest teacher and the only teacher. Hence, more things are caught than taught. Did you observe your parents, stepparents, or even grandparents apologizing and forgiving one another? After asking that question of thousands of spouses, I estimate that less than 2 percent of spouses responded "yes." So unfortunately, you may struggle because like most individuals you never learned as a child how to apologize and forgive.

Another contributing factor is low self-esteem. If you lack self-confidence, apologizing will be a challenge, because you may feel like a defect for even making a mistake and needing to apologize. Or when your spouse apologizes and you forgive them, due to low self-worth you may feel like your spouse is the superior partner. Yet, when you regularly apologize or forgive, you can actually enhance your self-esteem.

At times, you may resist forgiving because you possess the same shortcoming within yourself. For example, if your spouse apologizes for being impatient, your hesitation to forgive may come from your own personal impatience. And by withholding forgiveness, you are trumpeting to your spouse your own inner shortcoming of impatience.

Retaliation and revenge are never workable solutions for a satisfying marriage. It really makes no difference why forgiveness is problematic. Ultimately, just understanding the aforementioned obstacles associated with forgiveness may provide you with insights into the challenge. When either of you makes a mistake, you need to apologize in writing or verbally within twenty-four hours. And whenever your spouse apologizes, you need to forgive in order to heal your relationship and restore your oneness. Without *forgiveness*, it is nearly impossible to have personal happiness, and that usually results in relationship unhappiness as well.

4. SPONGES AND TEFLON

Please understand that frequently a difference exists between men and women when it comes to forgiveness. Books have been written about the gender differences between men and women. On the whole, men and women will view hurts and disappointments in contrasting ways. Generally speaking, a majority of women are *feelers* while most men are *thinkers*.

Being thinkers, most men are more like *Teflon* and think through "marital cuts" (See Lesson 5). For example, if I were to call a guy a "big dummy," but within a short period of time say, "I am sorry for calling you a big dummy, will you please forgive me?" after responding, "I forgive you," most men would not re-member the next day that I even called them a "big dummy." A guy, in Teflon fashion, would wash the Teflon pan, turn it side-ways, letting the water run off, and the pan would be dry in thirty minutes. Being called an unkind name would almost be a thing of the past.

However, being *feelers*, most women are like *sponges*, and that is why I have heard husbands state numerous times, "I can't be-lieve what my wife remembers from the past." Using my previous example, let's say I call a woman a "big dummy." Again, within a short period of time I apologize with, "I am sorry for calling you a big dummy, will you please forgive me?" After saying, "I forgive you" or "With God's help, I will work at forgiving you," the very next day, most ladies would still remember that I called them a "big dummy." A lady once told me that most women would not only recall the next day being called a "big dummy," but ten years later would still remember what I was wearing when I called them that harmful name.

When a marital "cut" occurs from a husband, most wives throw the *sponge* in a pail of water where it becomes sopping wet. After the husband apologizes and the wife responds with forgiveness, the sponge is pulled out of the pail and squeezed, but it still remains wet. The sponge will need to be squeezed many times before it is even somewhat dry. Forgiveness for *feel-ers* takes much more effort.

Certainly, this does not mean women are better than men due to an excellent memory, nor does it mean that men are better than women because they have a shorter memory. However, it does point out that men and women will handle forgiven wrongs in a different fashion.

Personally, whether you are *Teflon* or a *sponge*, please remem-ber the promise in Lesson 9: Once the "I forgive you" is pro-nounced, it is very unhealthy to bring the forgiven wrong up to your spouse ever again. For a satisfying marriage, both of you must agree that "letting go" is an essential attribute of a healthy Christian spouse.

5. SCRATCHES, CUTS, AND LACERATIONS

Too often I have counseled spouses where hurts and disappointments are broken into two categories: minor violations or major felonies. Such dichotomous or good-bad thinking can quickly damage a marriage, because that would mean every hurt or disappointment must be addressed—but this is not true.

Hence, dividing marital injuries into three categories can make a significant difference with relationship happiness. I use a medical model to explain the different types of hurts and disappointments within a relationship. Begin today to view marital hurts as *scratches*, *cuts*, and *lacerations*. Everyone has their own "personal" dictionary, so realize what is a *scratch* to one spouse may be regarded as a *cut* to the other partner.

A *marital scratch* is similar to scratching yourself while working around your house. You probably do not immediately treat the scratch, but instead just let it go. You realize that a scratch is very insignificant, will only leave a faint scab, and heal quickly on its own. *Don't stress over scratches!*

Likewise, your marriage will have numerous scratches that you will need to overlook, so let the scratches go. Stressing over scratches will only diminish your happiness. Even in gratifying marriages, scratches or minor irritations regularly occur. Every spouse has minor flaws and will accidentally *scratch* a spouse or marriage. By being lenient, merciful, and recognizing *marital scratches* as little annoyances, you avoid being a complaining nagger and daily dealing with problems. However, if you scratch the same skin area over and over again, that will now create a cut. So repetitive scratches cannot be ignored in a relationship but must be handled as cuts.

While physical scratches are not significant, physical cuts do require treatment. If you cut yourself while working in the yard, you will probably care for the cut with ointment and a bandage to prevent an infection. A cut is usually not only somewhat painful, but a lack of action can lead to an infection. For the sake of good physical health, you treat a cut, and similarly you will also want to care for *cuts in your marriage* through the apologizing and forgiving process.

In life, you will rarely receive a laceration. My definition of a laceration is a deep cut that requires stitches by a medical doctor. The stitches pull the skin together, similar to the way that apologizing and forgiving pull your relationship back together. Some examples of *marital lacerations* would be adultery, physical abuse, or severe verbal abuse. Lacerations and some cuts often leave scars, but thankfully when healing has occurred, that pain is part of the past.

Like physical cuts and lacerations, the good news is that *marital cuts* and *lacerations* can be healed through an apologizing and forgiving process. However, just as a medical doctor needs knowledge to treat physical lacerations, couples require knowledge for healing *marital lacerations*. Sadly, I estimate that 95 percent of spouses do not have that specific know-how to treat *marital cuts* and *lacerations*. However, I have great news: This chapter will provide the two of you with the necessary apologizing and forgiving wisdom to heal those cuts and lacerations.

6. REGULARLY LOOK IN THE MIRROR

Physically, a mirror can be utilized to show whether our face is dirty or what needs to be done to enhance our appearance. Likewise, Christians need to daily look in a *biblical mirror* at how thoughts, words, and actions may trespass against God's commandments. A *biblical mirror* is often referred to as the Law of God. Galatians 3:19 states, "Why, then, the Law [what was its purpose]? It was added [after the promise to Abraham, to reveal to people their guilt] because of transgressions [that is, to make people conscious of the sinfulness of sin]" (AMP). Although difficult, acknowledging sin is always the first step. Such a gaze into the "mirror of God" can expose ungodly or sinful behaviors and words. Without recognition of wrong, a repentant spirit will not be present, but that must happen before a confession or apology to God.

Likewise, a *marriage mirror* illuminates and brings to awareness damaging words and behaviors. If your spouse has made this comment about you, "You rarely say you are sorry for anything," your relationship will struggle. Wholesome spouses regularly look in the *marriage mirror* to see how their words and behaviors may have negatively impacted their spouse. A daily, honest self-appraisal creates an environment for valuable improvements leading to a rewarding marriage.

However, as a spouse, one of your most significant challenges will be to gaze in the *marriage mirror* at your comments and behaviors. It is essential that both of you are capable of evaluating your words and actions. If either you or your spouse cannot assess your harmful words and actions, it will be extremely difficult for your marriage to experience growth and satisfaction.

Answering two key questions can help you look in the mirror. One: "What would I LIKE about being married to myself?" And two: "What would I DISLIKE about being married to myself?" Don't just think about your responses, but actually write down on paper the enjoyable and distasteful aspects of being married to yourself.

In my practice, numerous spouses have done this exercise. The results have been eye-opening for many partners. I had one husband astonishingly state, "I could not find even one thing I would like about being married to me." Was it any surprise that his wife wanted to end the marriage?

So daily, enhance your relationship by *looking in the mirror.* Without each of you having the willingness to both gaze into a *marriage mirror* and then recognize any "dirt," hope for a gratifying marriage is lessened. Always show respect to your spouse by identifying your hurts and wrongs through a *marriage mirror.*

7. UNDERSTAND GUILT, SHAME, AND ACCOUNTABILITY

Genuine guilt is an emotional reaction to a specific word or behavior that offended your spouse. Guilt is usually associated with something said or done, although there can also be guilt over a sinful or wrongful thought. On the other hand, *shame* is more of a feeling that impacts our self-worth. Healthy shame helps us be humble, but most often shame causes a feeling that we are a "mistake," a "defect," or a "bad person." Spouses frequently confuse guilt and shame, creating an unhealthy atmosphere in the relationship. Distinguishing properly between *guilt* and *shame* is an important awareness for a satisfying marriage.

From a biblical perspective, disobeying any of the Ten Commandments should create a feeling of guilt. *Guilt* stems from either sinning against God or one's neighbor, and for a married individual, one's spouse is the closest neighbor. One of the best ways to help a marital relationship is for you to define together what violates God's laws and your marital rules so that you only address genuine guilt not shameful feelings. Having real *guilt* means accepting responsibility for one's wrongs.

From a secular perspective, *guilt* arises in a marriage when a spouse does something morally wrong to their partner or when a spouse does not meet reasonable expectations within a marital relationship by not demonstrating the same loyalty, support, and kindness shown to them. In a healthy marriage when a legitimate wrong has been committed, the offending spouse will experience guilt and apologize. When both of you are able to recognize and admit guilt for genuine offenses, you are on the road to a gratifying relationship.

From a practical perspective, guilt can only be addressed through apologizing and forgiving. For a gratifying marriage, having guilt for sinful or hurtful words and actions is a must. A wife once told me, "Frequently, my husband messes up, but he has no idea how he hurt me and our relationship." Certainly, you understand how dangerous that was for the future of their marriage.

Apologizing and forgiving addresses true *guilt*, not *shame*. If unhealthy shame is the culprit, it is not necessary for a spouse to repent and apologize. *Shame* is a feeling that "I am bad," rather than "I have done a bad thing," which is *guilt*. Shame sends a false message to the heart of our self-worth that we are failures in nearly every aspect of life and never acceptable to our spouse and others. Shame-based spouses generally: are excessively selfless; are people pleasers; have trouble accepting compliments; lack an ability to create emotional closeness; and have a difficult time nurturing a partner. A shame-based spouse must work hard to overcome dangerous shameful feelings, otherwise, the marital relationship will struggle in many aspects.

A healthy spouse will be *personally responsible* for wrongful words and actions and have genuine guilt feelings. Such legitimate guilt will initiate the apologizing and forgiving process. Just as important, a partner without toxic shame will hold their spouse accountable when experiencing hurts and disappointments. *Personal accountability* and *spousal accountability* are both essential for a satisfying marriage.

In the book of Genesis, we read just how difficult *personal accountability* was for Adam and Eve. When God approached Adam, rather than accept responsibility for his sin, Adam blamed God by saying, "The woman whom You gave to be with me—she gave me [fruit] from the tree" (Genesis 3:12 AMP). Likewise, Eve blamed her sin on Satan by saying, "The serpent beguiled and deceived me" (Genesis 3:13 AMP). Blaming your spouse for your unwholesome behavior rather than accepting responsibility for a harmful word or action is a detrimental weakness of a troubled marriage.

Just like God with Adam and Eve, you need to *hold your spouse accountable* for their marital injuries. After Adam and Eve sinned, God confronted them with their trespass. Likewise, when you experience marital sorrow, always let your spouse know your heartache. When you do not hold your spouse accountable, you only store up bitterness that can erode away your emotional connection.

I saw a Christian couple who faithfully worshiped every Sunday morning with their children. Everyone in their church felt they were the ideal Christian couple and family. However, this Christian husband was gone four nights per week, Monday through Thursday, almost year-round. During the summer, he was in two pickleball leagues and two golf leagues. During the winter, he was in two volleyball leagues and two bowling leagues.

This husband spent more time with his recreational sports activities than he did with his wife and children. They felt abandoned and neglected by his absence. The husband had neither guilt nor shame. The wife never shared her deep disappointment and pain, believing that her husband needed to recognize his selfish behaviors (see Lesson 47) on his own. Unfortunately, his wife found a coworker who gave her attention, spent time with her, and made her feel special. Sadly, their emotional friendship led to a physical affair and eventual divorce.

The husband was blind to his extreme selfishness, and the wife never held him accountable for his irresponsible, damaging behaviors. I am not excusing the wife's affair, but this is a prime example for this lesson. Had both spouses understood the importance of the *mirror for personal accountability* and *holding one's spouse accountable*, I truly believe that their divorce would never have happened.

First, always *accept personal responsibility* for your harmful actions by *looking in the mirror* at your harmful words and behaviors. Then make an authentic commitment to overcome your damaging words and behaviors. By being personally accountable, followed by an appropriate apology, you enhance your marriage and allow for a fresh start each morning.

Second, you must *hold your spouse accountable* when you are hurting on the inside from damaging actions. To withhold that you have been wronged will often create resentment and begin building a grudge wall. Often, your spouse is simply not aware how their actions have broken your heart. By holding your spouse accountable, you allow them to make the appropriate changes that can ensure a satisfying relationship, thus building up your marriage, not tearing it down.

So, when either of you lacks an understanding of *genuine guilt* or possesses *toxic shame*, emotional closeness will probably be absent. And just as damaging, when either of you is unable to look in the *mirror for personal accountability* or *hold your spouse accountable*, your relationship may be permeated with bitterness.

8. WHOLE CIRCLE OF FORGIVENESS: ALL THREE COMPONENTS ARE NECESSARY

The daily life of a Christian includes confessing to God for sins in thoughts, words, or actions. 1 John 1:9 states, "If we [freely] admit that we have sinned and confess our sins, God is faithful and just [true to His own nature and promises], and will forgive our sins and cleanse us continually from all unrighteousness [our wrongdoing, everything not in conformity with His will and purpose]" (AMP).

When a spouse does not have the habit of regularly repenting to God, what is also probably lacking is the habit of regularly apologizing to their partner. By daily confessing your sin to God, you develop an attitude of not wanting to sin against our Lord

God and your spouse. A godly, repentant attitude almost always carries over into your marital relationship. If both of you do not appropriately apologize and forgive one another, your marriage may be in a danger zone.

Three elements comprise the forgiveness process. All three components are essential for healing hurts and disappointments that will occur in even satisfying marriages. If any of the three are not utilized, your marriage will often struggle with varying degrees of emotional and relational suffering.

The first step is to say, *"I am sorry I hurt you by . . ."* I think it is good to use the word "hurt" when apologizing to your spouse because that indicates compassion as well as a desire to heal the broken relationship. It is also extremely important to be *specific* with your apology. For example, "I am so sorry I hurt you by calling you a name." No matter what, it is extremely important to develop the healthy habit of saying *"I am sorry I hurt you by . . . "*

You may also begin the forgiveness process through a note of apology with those same words. But if you apologize in writing, it is essential that you follow up with a verbal apology. An insight: To apologize is difficult for all of us, but it is particularly challenging for an insecure spouse.

Very few spouses even use the first step: *"I am sorry I hurt you by . . . "* Unfortunately, if you only say, "I am sorry," there is a tendency to be flippant and insincere with your tone of voice. Even when you don't agree that you committed a wrongful word or action, it is still important to apologize. In those situations, you apologize for hurt feelings. For example, if your partner believes you don't compliment enough, you would say, *"I am sorry I hurt your feelings* by not being appreciative," even though you may not agree. Then per chapter 6, discuss together your viewpoint regarding lack of compliments.

It is equally important to never use the word *but* because *but* is an eraser. When I say to someone, "You are a wonderful Christian person, but . . ." I just erased the initial comment:

"You are a wonderful Christian person." Unfortunately, I have frequently heard one spouse tell their partner, "I am sorry I hurt your feelings, but you did XYZ." Certainly, that is not a sincere apology.

The second step is seeking forgiveness with *"Will you please forgive me?"* Seeking forgiveness requires a great deal of courage and humility. Humility is *not* thinking about yourself, but only about your spouse and how you can heal your marriage through a loving request for forgiveness. Often, in a troubled marriage, the word *please* is omitted. The *"Will you **please** forgive me?"* indicates a repentant attitude and lets your spouse know that you are making a commitment to change.

Finally, God's Word says we are to *always forgive*, and that is the third step. Every spouse does well to follow Jesus' example in Luke 23:34: "Jesus said, 'Father, forgive them, for they do not know what they are doing'" (NIV). Hence, the Bible tells us to forgive no matter what, even if there is no repentance or even a request for forgiveness.

When your spouse has asked, *"Will you please forgive me?"* always reply with the word *forgive*. It is absolutely essential that you use the word *forgive* and not just say, "That's okay," or "I'm over it," or "No big deal," or "Whatever." To hear your spouse say either *"I forgive you"* or *"With God's help, I will work at forgiving you"* completes the whole circle of forgiveness.

An apology for a cut may only necessitate an *"I forgive you."* However, when there is intense suffering and pain from a laceration, after an apology the response may be *"With God's help, I will work at forgiving you."* A betrayed spouse whose partner was sexually unfaithful may find it extremely difficult to even utter the phrase, *"With God's help, I will work at forgiving you"* much less to say, *"I forgive you."* Thus, the phrase *"With God's help, I will work at forgiving you"* will still allow the process of forgiveness to take hold because hearing the word *forgive* completes the whole *circle of forgiveness.*

Only God can forgive and remember sin no more. So unbelievably God absolutely forgets! Isaiah 43:25 declares, "I, only I am He who wipes out your transgressions for My own sake, and I will not remember your sins" (AMP). As humans, we do forgive, but we remember and almost never forget.

For every spouse, apologizing and forgiving can often be an exhausting, demanding journey. However, your efforts will create a caring, compassionate heart and a strong marital connection. And most importantly, your marriage will be happier because both of you are experts at implementing the whole *circle of forgiveness*:

1. "I am sorry I hurt you by . . ."
2. "Will you please forgive me?"
3. Forgive by saying:
    a. "I forgive you" or
    b. "With God's help, I will work at forgiving you."

9. FORGIVENESS IS A GIFT, A PROMISE, AND A PROCESS

A GIFT

Romans 6:23 tells us that "the free gift of God [that is, His remarkable, overwhelming gift of grace to believers] is eternal life through Christ Jesus our Lord" (AMP). Through faith in Jesus Christ, Christians are forever forgiven and receive God's *gift* of eternal life. Likewise, forgiveness is absolutely the best *gift* that you can ever give your spouse. However, forgiveness is also the most difficult gift you will ever give your spouse. And forgiveness is perhaps the last gift on your mind after you have experienced a hurt. In every marriage, grace or undeserved kindness must abound because sometimes you will need forgiveness and other times you will need to grant forgiveness to your spouse.

Almighty God hates sin, and to forgive sin He had to give the ultimate *gift*, sacrificing the Son of God, Jesus Christ. The Son of

God was beaten, a crown of thorns placed on His head, and then Jesus was nailed to the rugged cross. If it is that hard for our heavenly Father to provide the gift of forgiveness, will it ever be an easy task for you to forgive your spouse? Of course, the answer is an absolute NO.

Nonetheless, due to Jesus Christ's death and resurrection, God forgave the sins of the world. Thus, God gave the world the greatest gift ever, and that wonderful *gift*, the forgiveness of sins, leads to eternal life in heaven. In your marital relationship, forgiveness is a *double gift*, since you also grant yourself a gift by not dwelling on the offense.

After your spouse has apologized and sought your forgiveness, for the sake of Jesus Christ you can give them a *gift* of forgiveness, the greatest *marital gift* you will ever give your partner. Hopefully, by thinking about God's costly gift for you, that concept will make it somewhat easier for you to say either *"I forgive you"* or *"With God's help, I will work at forgiving you."* When your spouse apologizes and seeks your forgiveness, and you declare, *"I forgive you,"* you truly begin understanding the grace, mercy, and everlasting love of God for you.

A PROMISE

Forgiveness is a spiritual and verbal function, not a biological or mental function. When you forgive your spouse, you almost never forget the offense because only almighty God forgives and forgets! In Psalm 103:12 we are given the thought: "As far as the east is from the west—that is how far he (God) has removed our rebellious acts from himself" (GW). However, for us as humans, forgiveness is *promising* not to bring up the forgiven wrong to your spouse ever again.

For example, I could ask you to forget the terrorist attacks in New York City on September 11, 2011. However, it is absolutely impossible to erase that painful memory from your mind. The traumatic images of those planes flying into the Twin Towers, the fires, numerous individuals in chaos, all are deeply engrained in your brain. Hopefully, you have forgiven the terrorists for their confused, unhealthy thinking that led to the deaths of thousands of innocent people, but you will never forget the horror. Likewise, once your spouse has repented, asked for forgiveness, and been granted your gift of forgiveness, you agree never to bring up that forgiven wrong again.

Develop a short memory and absolutely avoid grudges by *promising* yourself that you will not dwell on the forgiven hurt. Once you have forgiven your partner, commit to never again either reminding them of or using that offense against your spouse. In addition, you *promise* to not tell family or friends about your partner's offense. Thus, you are *promising* not to ever use the forgiven hurt against your spouse in any way.

A PROCESS

When you forgive your spouse, especially for a laceration, your forgiveness is really a *process* that may last a lifetime. Forgiving a laceration may feel like a grinding, uphill, rocky journey that seems to go on forever.

When adultery, physical abuse, or extreme verbal abuse occurs, and even after your spouse repents and commits to never repeating that offense again, it will be difficult to forgive your spouse and move forward in the marriage. For the rest of your life, it may be a daily *process*, where you find it necessary to say to yourself every morning, "With God's help, I am working at forgiving you, and I am moving forward in our relationship."

Forgiveness for your marriage is like lubrication for your car. Without forgiveness, friction would eventually kill your "marriage engine." Forgiveness greases all the hurts and disappointments throughout your relationship, allowing your "marital car" to run smoothly.

Philippians 3:13 declares, "Forgetting what lies behind and straining forward to what lies ahead" (ESV). Hence, with the *process* of forgiveness, it may be necessary to say to yourself, "It is okay to look back, but I will not stare because I have forgiven my spouse." While driving your car, if you stare in your rearview mirror rather than look forward through the windshield, you will probably crash your car. Likewise for *lacerations*: Recognize that forgiveness may be a lifelong, daily *process*. When you forgive, you are focused on the future for a more satisfying relationship.

10. FIRST REPENT, SECOND INCREASE TRUST

As explained in Lesson 2, in order for reconciliation to occur, a spouse must always repent and begin making changes in a positive direction. So, *repentance* always happens first, and that allows the next step of *rebuilding trust*.

Proverbs 3:5 declares, "Trust in and rely confidently on the Lord with all your heart, and do not rely on your own insight or understanding" (AMP). You can have 100 percent trust in God, complete trust in all of God's promises in the Bible, and through faith in Jesus have confident trust in your heavenly home.

However, no spouse ever has or ever will be 100 percent trustworthy. King David was a "man after God's own heart" (see Acts 13:22), and he committed adultery and murder, major lacerations to his marriage. After a serious marital cut or a laceration, sadly I have heard hundreds of times, "I thought I could trust my spouse 100 percent." Belatedly, those spouses realized that such a faulty assessment of trust led to serious trouble.

Trust actually falls on a continuum from 1 percent to 99 percent. For almost every happy marriage, *trust* is usually in the 90th percentile, and of course, the closer to 99 percent, the better it is for your marriage.

Having a forgiving spirit with spousal offenses is a Christlike behavior. As explained in Lesson 9, forgiveness is a gift that you freely give to your spouse. Almighty God desires every spouse to always forgive, but complete reconciliation is optional, depending upon repentance, a change of ways, as well as *words and actions that rebuild trust*. Forgiveness does not equal trust, and thus forgiveness may not necessarily restore your relationship. Thus, you need to always forgive your spouse, but a spouse must earn *trust* through restorative actions in order to renew a marital relationship.

For example, if Paul commits adultery but does not ask for forgiveness, Pam would be a healthy spouse by following Jesus' example and forgiving Paul. However, Pam's forgiveness will probably not restore the marital relationship until Paul repents, changes his ways by breaking off the affair, and begins to rebuild *trust*. After a laceration like adultery, *repentance must occur,* and *trust must be earned* before a marriage can have a fresh new start. Hence, Paul repents by changing his unfaithful ways, and then rebuilds the broken *trust through restorative words and actions.*

It is a good idea for Pam to make a specific, written list of actions and words that could rebuild her *trust* in Paul. Only when Pam is 90-plus percent confident in trusting Paul's faithfulness will their marriage have a chance for reconciliation. Hence, *repentance* and *trust* must be present for the possibility of reconciliation, as explained in Lesson 11.

11. RECONCILIATION: THE ULTIMATE GOAL

The Bible encourages reconciliation for our relationships, primarily with God but also others. 2 Corinthians 5:18 states, "Now all these things are from God, who reconciled us to Himself through Christ and gave us the ministry of reconciliation" (NKJV). *Reconciliation* is the positive behavioral result, while apologizing and forgiving initiates the healing process. The only avenue for resolving hurts and disappointments is the apologizing and forgiving process that concludes in reconciliation. Without *reconciliation*, the two of you will have difficulty restoring your emotional connection for a satisfying marriage.

Again, the components that produce the restoration of a broken marital bond are *repenting* or a change of ways, *apologizing, forgiving*, and rebuilding *trust*. In your marriage, when an offender repents and changes their ungodly ways, and the offended offers forgiveness, a rewarding restoration is generally the result. *Reconciliation* provides that fresh start, a new beginning, for a rich, rewarding marital relationship.

Unfortunately, *reconciliation* may not always be the outcome following apologizing and forgiving. For example, the crucifiers of Jesus did not apologize, much less repent by removing the nails, and so there was no reconciliation. Likewise in a marriage, restoration of the relationship may not be possible for several reasons. For example, the offending spouse may be unaware of inflicting pain on their partner; extreme verbal abuse may be constant; domestic violence may be ongoing; the offending spouse may refuse to make positive, godly changes; and a pattern of damaging behavior may continue on a regular basis.

Before reconciling your marital connection, wait for repentance and a lengthy pattern of truthful words and honest actions by your spouse. Full *reconciliation* is not possible, nor is it recommended, if *repentance* and *trust* are not present. Hopefully, in your marriage, the two of you will always be able to repent, apologize, forgive, and rebuild trust, so you can open the *reconciliation* door for a happy, satisfying relationship.

12. TWO REPENTANT, FORGIVING SPOUSES EQUAL ONE GRATIFYING MARRIAGE

Mistakes happen in every satisfying marriage! Yet every happy Christian couple resolves heartaches and painful experiences through *repenting, apologizing, forgiving*, and rebuilding *trust*, for a positive reconciliation outcome resulting in a stronger relationship. The Bible states, "Blessed [spiritually calm with life-joy in God's favor] are the makers and maintainers of peace" (Matthew

5:9 AMP). A peacemaking spouse is intent on reconciliation in order to maintain marital satisfaction.

So, be like Jesus and take a compassionate, merciful view of your spouse, realizing that everyone is an imperfect sinner. God looks at us through love in Jesus Christ, likewise look at your spouse through kind and patient eyes so that you are continually developing your forgiving spirit.

Every satisfying marriage is a union of two wonderful *forgivers*. As long as you are able to *repent, apologize* to one another, and *forgive* each other, the probabilities for a satisfying marriage increase immensely.

Your marriage will only be gratifying when both of you strive to understand the concepts and process of *reconciliation*, which initially flows from a heart of *forgiveness*. At times, you will be the one needing to receive mercy and grace, while other times you will need to bestow mercy and grace upon your spouse. When you and your spouse are able to apologize and forgive each other, you significantly increase the probabilities for a glimpse of heavenly bliss.

I have never seen even one satisfying marriage that did not have *two spouses willing to apologize and forgive to heal hurts.* Hence, gratification equals *two awesome apologizers* as well as *two fantastic forgivers!* By always apologizing and forgiving each other, your hurts will be healed, and your relationship will be restored. Develop the skills discussed in this opening chapter, and you most likely will not need to worry about your marital future.

CHAPTER II

THE FOUR PRACTICAL WISDOM HABITS

cclesiastes 3 declares: "To everything there is a season . . . a time to embrace . . . a time to love," and there is a season or time for *talking* and *touching* within every happy marriage. Matthew 5:16 instructs Christians to "let your light shine before men in such a way that they may see your good deeds and moral excellence" (AMP). The *four basic habits* are one of the best ways for showing daily commitment to your spouse through four forms of good works for enhancing your emotional and spiritual oneness.

Although only a starting point, these *four practical wisdom habits*—making eye contact while talking each day, hugging, kissing, and spending time together—are the foundation for maintaining relational and biblical oneness. These are not a "rocket science" discovery. Yet these simple behaviors are absolutely essential for a satisfying relationship.

They're also often the first to slide away. Think back to when you were dating—back then, you probably spent hours touching and talking with each other. Unfortunately, after a few years of marriage, for many couples these activities have almost evaporated. Complacency is usually the first step toward a failed marriage, and certainly a lack of these four habits increases the destructiveness of complacency.

Talking and touching are what create true romance. It's what helped you fall in love and created the powerful emotional bond that led you to the decision to marry. When these pillars get stronger, your marriage will immediately improve, as will your connection.

How easy are the *four basic habits*? You only need to spend *10 minutes* on the first three combined! And a date can be almost any activity and need only happen every other week. At first, to remind yourself, you might place a note about them on your refrigerator or bathroom mirror. In time, they'll go back to being routine.

13. SPEND TEN MINUTES TALKING, EYE TO EYE

The Bible states, "The eye is the lamp of the body" (Matthew 6:22 AMP). Your entire face can effectively communicate messages with your spouse, but *your eyes* hold the most significance. Your *eyes* are the windows to your heart! And even the Lord God "looks at the heart" (1 Samuel 16:7 AMP). When you look into your partner's eyes—and when he or she looks in yours—you are establishing a "heart connection." *Looking into each other's eyes* absolutely warms your hearts. Warming each other's hearts creates a solid emotional bond.

An excellent synonym for *love* is *time*. Due to very little time together, too many couples seek to end their relationship. Having time together does not absolutely guarantee success, but time together increases the odds of achieving a fulfilling marriage. The likelihood of a rich, rewarding marriage is slim to none without mutual commitment for positive eye-to-eye time together. Make your marriage a priority and spend ten minutes of daily *time* or *love* with your spouse!

When you were first dating, daily intentional *eye-to-eye contact* was a given. And before marriage, when you regularly shared your hearts with each other, you knew everything about your spouse's heart and life. Sure, there may have also been communication by phone, text message, e-mail, or "snail" mail. But it was being in the presence of the other that conveyed your love. As you looked into each other's eyes intensely and often, you felt sincerely valued and deeply loved. Sharing your hearts demonstrated care, and that caring action of looking into each other's eyes prompted a deep sense of trust and commitment in the one you love.

I believe the vast majority of couples in the United States do not have *eye-to-eye heart talks* even once per month. Too many spouses have more eye-to-eye contact with others rather than their partner, a situation that is perilous to a marriage, too often leading to affairs. Initially I ask struggling couples to tell me the last time they had ten uninterrupted minutes of consistent eye-to-eye contact. Invariably the response runs from "rarely" to "I can't remember."

Unintentionally, after a few married years, most couples diminish emotional intimacy by simply not talking with each other *eye-to-eye*. This regular lack of sustained eye contact can lead your hearts to eventually become stone-cold. Sadly, the colder your hearts become, the more complacent you become in your relationship. Complacency then leads to more bad habits and a downward spiral toward deterioration.

Communication between a husband and a wife is primary, and that usually happens through scheduled time together. I am not suggesting a timed ten-minute conversation. Instead the goal is meaningful minutes of *looking into each other's eyes*. I also realize that ten minutes of simply staring at each other will not guarantee a successful marriage. But intentional, uninterrupted eye contact, accompanied by winsome and caring words, is a vital element to staying emotionally joined over the long haul. When you make *frequent, loving eye contact*, you automatically begin to intimately bond with one another.

Despite the fact that we use our eyes every waking moment, spending ten minutes a day in this kind of contact with your spouse does not come naturally. It is a practice that takes practice! Here are some suggested guidelines: Select a location that ensures you have each other's full attention; an intimate physical distance is eighteen to twenty-four inches, so have that proximity as a goal when you sit down together; some spouses hold hands to enhance their connection even more; and sit so you can look directly into your partner's eyes. The intent for these few minutes is to have a pleasant, encouraging interaction. Think of it as a lighthearted coffee conversation. Take turns speaking and never interrupt. Listen with your inner being by giving undivided attention to communicate that your spouse is so very important.

Next, remove all distractions. Turn off the television and music gadgets, put aside your cell phones, newspaper, magazine, or anything else that might distract you. Removing distractions allows for establishing an emotional connection. You might begin by sharing two good things that happened to you that day or marital goals for the weekend or even dreams about the future.

Never, never, never discuss problems during this *heart connection* time! When you discuss troublesome issues about home repairs, frustrations with coworkers, financial stress, or other difficulties, these ten minutes you look forward to will quickly deteriorate into ten minutes you always want to avoid! Driving together in the car or cooking in the kitchen together are natural times to talk, but they don't really allow for full focus. Eating together at the table is important for marital communication, but that also does not amply produce your special heart conversation.

Ask yourself, "When do I most enjoy talking with my spouse?" Perhaps decide together each Sunday what days will allow for you to have your "heart talks." During your *eye-to-eye heart talks*, you may want to read a lesson from *Simple Habits for Marital Happiness* and discuss the knowledge gained for building a pleasing relationship.

Ideally it would be wonderful to spend seventy minutes per week in eye-to-eye discussions, but that is usually not realistic. When no children are in the home, five days per week is actually a reasonable goal. When children are in the home, hopefully you can spend three out of seven days, thirty minutes per week, in bonding your hearts together. Strive for seventy minutes every week but have grace in your relationship and understand that even thirty minutes per week will make a significant difference.

A healthy axiom for a strong marriage is "Talk and talk some more!" I am not suggesting a regular *ten-minute eye-to-eye heart talk* is the magical pill for ensuring a successful marriage. But a few minutes of *uninterrupted eye contact* goes a long way toward creating emotional intimacy, and thus preventing you from becoming complacent and distant. Developing a regular time for your *ten-minute eye-to-eye* conversation will solidly help connect your hearts for a lifetime. And a regular "heart connection" tells your spouse that you value him or her, and you are willing to strengthen your relationship.

14. HUG FOR TEN SECONDS

When the Prodigal Son returned home, what was most meaningful for his father was a significant hug. The father of the Prodigal Son "ran and **embraced him** and kissed him (the son)" (Luke 15:20 AMP). When you were dating, hugging was a natural, simple habit that bonded you together and frequently occurred either when you greeted each other or said good-bye to each other. Before marriage you probably thought, "I absolutely love physical touch from my partner and look forward to hugging my future spouse for a lifetime." The reason is those *lengthy hugs* connected your hearts and minds together! Affection is the cement for your marriage.

Numerous research studies have proven that touch enhances a person's physical health and emotional well-being. Some of the physical benefits include releasing the "feel-good" chemical oxytocin, lowering your blood pressure, improving your mood, diminishing pain, and reducing stress. Touch is also enormously important for your marriage. Daily hugs, holding hands, and sitting together are indispensable "touching" behaviors for your marital satisfaction.

After a few years of marriage, expressing affection is not a normal practice for many spouses and rarely is it spontaneous. When the marital foundation begins to crack, a *long-lasting hug* is perhaps one of the first habits that can evaporate. Unfortunately, some spouses were rarely touched as children or the touch they did receive was unhealthy, creating an awkward feeling of dread when they are touched. If that happened to you, remember to become comfortable being uncomfortable as you practice touching or hugging your spouse on a daily basis. If physical touch is absent, your relationship will often experience emotional distance, sexual intimacy problems, and a slide toward destruction.

What can you do to improve your hugs? Both good-bye and hello hugs are a beginning. In the morning, give each other a quick "brother-sister" good-bye hug as you separate for the day. A brother-sister hug is similar to the brief hug that happens between adult siblings at the holidays.

However, when you "meet and greet" one another each evening, a *ten-second hello hug* is absolutely essential for reconnecting with one another. At the end of the day, this ten-second physical embrace creates a warm, secure feeling as well as establishing a positive atmosphere for the evening.

Of course, I am not suggesting that you time your hugs. The goal is a *meaningful hug* versus the brother-sister variety. One couple who dramatically improved their marriage told me they were no longer "BSing" each other but only "HWing" one another. I was totally puzzled and asked what "BSing" meant. The wife replied, "No more 'brother-sister' hugs. Now we only give meaningful husband-wife hugs."

For many non-hugging couples, groping is the primary obstacle to this most basic habit. Thus, husbands take note! When giving a *ten second hug* never "grope"—that is, no "private touching" of any kind. I have had hundreds of wives tell me, "Dr. Schroeder, thank you for the 'no groping' guideline, because groping was the primary reason I hesitated to give my husband a hug."

In addition, I caution you husbands not to think that these daily hugs will lead to the bedroom. Otherwise, I can almost guarantee that this essential practice will not become a reality for the two of you. Simple non-groping, *lengthy hugs* every day will often improve your sexual intimacy. However, that is absolutely not the goal! Increasing your oneness is the objective.

Although physical touching sounds simple, when *lengthy hugs* have been absent for a while, one or both of you may be fearful to begin again. Overcoming the fear of prolonged hugs may require much practice before it becomes natural. Touch is probably the greatest way to emotionally connect with your spouse. Begin now, to not only boost your physical health but also your emotional closeness with your spouse through *meaningful hugs*.

15. GIVE A TEN-SECOND KISS

For most couples, *kissing* was the initial intimate moment in their relationship. Solomon begins the Song of Solomon, his book on marital love, by stating in the opening verse: "May he kiss me with the kisses of his mouth!" [Solomon arrives, she turns to him, saying] 'For your love is better than wine'" (Song of Solomon 1:2 AMP). This is the only romantic kiss spoken of in the Bible. Nonetheless, kissing in the Bible signifies a profound regard and esteem for another person. One of the most common ways to express love and admiration for your spouse is through a kiss. Perhaps the best assessment for your marital connection and love for each other is how frequently and intently, not passionately, you *kiss* one another.

Before marriage, you and your spouse probably passionately kissed each other on a regular basis. *Kissing* emotionally connected you together! *Kissing* created fond feelings and excitement because of the closeness of your eyes, nose, and of course, the touching of your lips. Most likely, *kissing* was pleasurable and enjoyable for both of you.

Sadly, after the early years of marriage, for many couples the initial enjoyable behavior of fervently kissing one another begins to diminish. Pecks become the norm, and that only diminishes your emotional bond and strong connection. What begins to predominate is the "brother-sister" kiss. As mentioned in the last chapter, a brother-sister kiss is defined as a quick peck greeting between adult siblings at Thanksgiving or Christmas. Unfortunately, when simple *lingering kisses* diminish, sexual intimacy often declines rapidly as well.

Due to the early morning rush of preparing to depart for the day, a brother-sister kiss is acceptable as the first spouse leaves home. However, at the end of the day, a significant *lingering kiss* of approximately ten seconds reconnects the two of you. To have a simple *lingering kiss of ten seconds* also reinforces your commitment and love for one another. Remember the two mantras: "Behaviors first, feelings follow" and "Do healthy motions, to change my emotions."

If your marriage is significantly troubled, one or both spouses often have difficulty with even a quick kiss. If that is your situation, I suggest just the ten-second hug without a kiss. After days of meaningful hugs, then begin a peck for several days so eventually the lingering kiss can begin reestablishing your emotional connection.

In addition, with a struggling marriage, I frequently hear one spouse say, "I am so tired of always initiating hugs and kisses." So, on the even dates the wife initiates the hug and kiss while the odd dates are the husband's days for initiation. Both of you are then accountable for a strong, satisfying marriage.

Kissing each other is really good for both of you because endorphins are automatically released, causing you to feel relaxed and also increasing your energy. A soft, lengthy kiss at the "meet and greet" time of day also makes a significant difference in setting a positive atmosphere for your evenings together. When you and your spouse connect daily with a *lingering kiss,* you strengthen your love for each other. As one couple shared, "It is astounding how simple, *lengthy kisses* and *hugs* improved our relationship." Today, begin giving each other *meaningful hugs* and *lingering kisses!*

16. DATE YOUR MATE—AND HERE'S WHAT COUNTS AS A DATE

The book of Proverbs is filled with godly, practical wisdom. Although *date your mate* is not found in the Bible, similar to practical, proverbial wisdom, it is one essential habit for every happy couple. One opening question I usually ask couples in their first counseling session is, "When was the last time you did something enjoyable together outside your home, without another couple, without children, and that wasn't a church or business activity?" Usually, the answer is "we can't remember" or "a long time ago." Almost immediately, the couple understands one reason they are experiencing heartache. At the same time, they also recognize that one of the essential habits, spending alone time with your mate, needs to be implemented immediately in order to develop a gratifying marriage.

Many couples are vaguely aware of advice that they should "date" their spouse on a regular basis. But few understand just how important it is, how to spend time together in a way that builds up their relationship (rather than time that devolves into arguments), and what exactly constitutes a date.

My definition of a *date* is at least one enjoyable hour of time outside the home with only the two of you. If you have no children in your home, I recommend that you go on a date every week. For those couples needing child care, depending on their age, I advocate a target of dating twice per month.

Some spouses often overspend on purchases, including dates, creating financial stress rather than a marital connection. So, I suggest you divide dates into "expensive" and "inexpensive" dates that have maximum spending limits. The goal is not to spend the allotted sum of money, but instead to minimize anxiety due to the fear of a spouse potentially overspending on a date. Setting a limit for each date allows you to stay within your monthly budget. Every household income is different, so the two of you will need to discuss and decide together your maximum amounts.

For example, if you have no children, perhaps you can afford $100 per month, or if you have children, the allotted amount will be whatever you can afford on a monthly basis. For example, you might agree that an expensive date cannot exceed $35 and an inexpensive one has a $15 maximum. A couple with children might try to exchange babysitting with another couple to minimize expenses.

When I suggest that you *date your mate*, most spouses normally think of a Friday or Saturday night dinner at 6:00 p.m., and they tell me they are "too busy." However, be creative, as a date does not necessarily have to be in the evening. Select a lunch together, a banana split on Saturday afternoon, or a stroll through the mall on a Sunday afternoon.

To remove power struggles, I suggest the husband make the first date selection, an expensive date. Then, the wife decides on an inexpensive outing. Continue alternating selections for future fun times.

In addition, I suggest when it's your turn to select a date, that you always choose an activity that will foster complete happiness within your spouse. When you are picking the activity, you are the *giver*. Although you may not necessarily be ecstatic about the date, you are hopefully still joyful because of the opportunity to provide a special time for your spouse.

One husband, whose wife liked romantic movies, selected a chick flick on his date night to provide a rewarding experience and make her feel special. His wife, for her date selection, took him to a baseball game because he was an avid baseball fan. Both husband and wife sacrificed their interests in order to value their spouse. The result—having a happy partner—made the giving spouse feel wonderful, and they both had a great time!

When you are responsible for the date, you cover all the details, contacting the restaurant for reservations, finding a babysitter, etc. Your goal is to allow your spouse to totally enjoy the occasion as you connect with each other.

Remember, you do not need to spend a dime on any date, even the "expensive" ones. Some couples have just gone for a walk in the park or a bike ride. One couple who had been married twenty years went fishing in a boat for two hours. They spent zero dollars. I do not recall if they caught any fish, but I do remember both of them telling me, "That was the best time we have had together in ten years."

I saw another couple where the husband knew his wife absolutely loved flying kites as a little girl. On one date, without her knowledge, he purchased two inexpensive kites and they flew kites together for two hours. It was not only an enjoyable activity for the wife, but one of their most memorable experiences together.

One couple with children had the great idea of having breakfast on a Saturday morning because it was easier to find a teenage babysitter. Starting in January, this couple went to twenty-six different breakfast restaurants every other Saturday morning for a year. Those weekends always began on a positive note, and they had a very gratifying twelve months. I am confident that you will come up with your own unique *date your mate* experiences.

Furthermore, at times you might add mystery to your dating experiences by not telling your partner where you are going, but only informing them how to dress for the event. As an example, several years ago I saw a couple who had an 11:30 a.m. counseling appointment in July. It was the husband's turn that month to pick an expensive date. The night before the session, he told his wife, "When we go see Dr. Schroeder tomorrow, wear shorts and tennis shoes because we are going on a special mystery date after the session."

Of course, his wife was ecstatic for several reasons. First, she felt so loved by her husband due to his planning of what she thought was an expensive date. Second, she was happy because the date was a big surprise. Third, she had fun trying to figure out where he was taking her.

The next morning, she happily put on her shorts and tennis shoes. She excitedly looked forward to the date and continued to have positive feelings for her husband due to his thoughtfulness. Right before they got in the car to attend the counseling session, the husband placed a picnic basket in the car that he had prepared in private. One of the wife's favorite activities in life was going on a picnic, and she was now on cloud nine. She really appreciated the mystery, joy, and excitement that began the previous night and carried over into the next day.

When you go on a date, your entire time from start to finish should have only "problem-free" conversation. Before I suggested this guideline, some couples reported having huge arguments on dates. One spouse told me they went out to eat, and before the meal came to the table, the other partner brought up an issue resulting in a significant conflict. Angry at each other, they paid for their meal and took the food home as a carryout.

Another spouse shared that they had a great time driving to the date and during the date, but on the way home, the other partner addressed a relationship problem and a major argument escalated in the car. So instead of a stronger connection, their relationship was even more emotionally distant. Each gave the other the silent treatment for several days. So, on dates, don't discuss any personal issues or even complaints about life, others, or your relationship. Your goal is positive, casual dialogue.

Lastly, because most couples rarely go on dates, when they do it is frequently to the exact same place. I recommend not doing the exact same date for several months, or at least alternating types of dates, because variety makes them even more enjoyable.

Starting this month, inject that same pleasure you experienced dating before you were married into your present relationship. Just like during your dating days, when the two of you do something fun together in a neutral environment away from home, the benefits are exponential. Almost any positive one-on-one time outside the home with your spouse leads to bonding. Bring enjoyment back to your marriage by making *date your mate* a habit!

CHAPTER III

HABITS THAT PROMOTE SPIRITUAL AND EMOTIONAL CLOSENESS

From the very first book of the Bible, Genesis, we learn that God desires husbands and wives to "become one flesh" and continually seek godly ways to promote spiritual closeness. The first lesson in this chapter, "Prayer and Worship," is a main Christian mission for the two of you. Colossians 4:2 encourages, "Be persistent and devoted to prayer" (AMP). Psalm 84:4 declares, "Blessed are those who dwell in your house" (NIV). When prayer and worship are regular, then your "marital house" is serving the Lord (see Joshua 24:15), and the result will most likely be a blessed marriage.

Spiritual closeness leads the way in establishing "oneness," but *emotional togetherness* is also essential for a rewarding relationship. *Marital emotional closeness* is similar to a water tower in a small town. Water flows out of the tower and puts the pressure in the faucets. At the same time that water is flowing out of the tower, water is also being pumped back in. If a town's water tower becomes empty and dry, people in that town have two choices. One, they could continue to live in the town and be perpetually irritated because they have to make weekly trips to the next town to purchase gallons and gallons of bottled water. Or they could move to a different town, because water is absolutely necessary for drinking, bathing, washing dishes, etc., and living in this town is just too difficult.

Likewise, both of you must pump water into your marriage water tower on a daily basis, or it will become empty. To have an empty marriage water tower creates friction, tension, and irritations for your relationship—and at worst, it can lead to a desire to move on. The *closeness habits* in this chapter keep your marriage water tower full.

A satisfying marriage is built through daily, respectful, two-way communication. These *Simple Habits* will help you quickly regenerate an emotional connection. You'll understand your spouse's inner life; feel sympathy and empathy for each other; and openly share feelings, thoughts, ideas, dreams, and goals, with no "wall" between the two of you. When a couple is emotionally connected, they usually have at least a four-to-one ratio of positive interactions to negative ones.

With emotionally distant couples, tension is often present, and minor irritations quickly become major arguments. When your marriage water tower is full, you are warmly bonded, resulting in less conflict between the two of you. Life's minor problems remain just that—annoyances that are easy to get past.

Use the loving behaviors in this closeness chapter to value your spouse and keep your marriage water tower full. When both of you learn how to demonstrate godly words and actions on a daily basis, marital bliss becomes a reality! So, view the lessons in this closeness chapter as opportunities to appreciate your spouse each day—a true privilege, not an obligation! You will find that valuing your partner allows you to become happier, too.

17. PRAYER AND WORSHIP

The utmost personal joy is always found in God alone. Likewise, a Christian marriage will experience the greatest happiness when both spouses are growing together in their faith in Jesus. A home built on the love of God found in Jesus Christ has a greater likelihood for a satisfying marriage. Psalm 127:1 states, "Unless the Lord builds the house, they labor in vain who build it" (AMP). Unfortunately, I have found that a truly difficult subject for a couple to discuss is faith in Jesus. Yet, living out your faith in a God-pleasing fashion is so very important for both of you. Hence, I believe an important goal is for you to find common ground with your faith in Christ, as well as a mutually agreed upon church home.

Praying aloud together at various times on a daily basis is not only important for your relationship with almighty God, but also for your marital union.

In terms of *prayer*, the apostle Paul encourages us to "pray without ceasing." *Prayer* is not an event, but a way of life. An intimate bond develops when both of you lift your voice to God at different times each day. God wants to hear your heart, and when you share your hearts together with God, you open your heart to each other, as well. Couples are often more satisfied when they pray together, because spouses are drawn together with a mutual focus on almighty God.

Yet, if you are like most couples, praying out loud extemporaneously by either one of you can be difficult because this was just not a part of your upbringing. A lack of praying out loud is often due to not knowing "how to" pray. Thus, *prayer together* does not come easily.

Let me suggest a three-part formula. The first step is to address God with "Dear heavenly Father" or "Almighty God" or simply "Dear God." The second step is to thank God for His blessings and to make requests for others and yourself. Finally, conclude with "in Jesus' name. Amen." Since Jesus is our Mediator, always conclude with "in Jesus' name," because Christ intercedes for us and delivers all of our prayers to our heavenly Father. An example prayer would be, "Dear God, thank You for our food and home. In Jesus' name. Amen."

Daily, I encourage you to practice *praying together* out loud by using the three-part formula. Then, each of you will take turns saying a prayer every other day. To remove some pressure, limit yourself to one sentence in the second part. Only when you feel comfortable should you add a second, third, or even more sentences in the second part.

As mentioned in chapter 2, most couples find it difficult to schedule even three ten-minute *eye-to-eye heart talks* per week. Hence, praying together can be equally as difficult for your schedule. Nonetheless, develop the practice of praying before every meal along with brief spontaneous prayers throughout the week.

If praying together is difficult, devotions will be even more of a challenge. However, having devotions as a couple can help establish your godly connection. An achievable goal would be to read a single passage from the New Testament and aim to discuss that Scripture for only a couple of minutes. If you want to discuss for a longer period of time, that is fine, but setting a maximum of a few minutes removes pressure. Then, one of you conclude the devotion time with a prayer. Again, you only need to say one sentence in the second part of the three-step formula.

Finding the right church home can be difficult. As you evaluate different churches, consider beliefs about the Bible, belief that Jesus Christ is the only way to eternal life in heaven with almighty God, baptism, style of worship, type of music, stance on Holy Communion, the church's programs, various times for worship, and even distance from your home. You want to be able to look forward to your church attendance because worshiping God together unites you as a couple. Both of you must feel comfortable with your eventual church home selection.

Finally, if either of you is not a Christian, PLEASE do not force your faith, because that will hurt your relationship and probably push your spouse further away from Jesus. Realize that it will do little good to try to convert your spouse with words.

For the believing spouse, your most important influence is your Christian walk, setting an example in speech, in life, in love, in faith, and in purity (see 1 Timothy 4:12). What your spouse observes by your faith is more important than what you say. So, the practice of your Christian faith means more than your talk. Simply be an example by living out your faith.

Certainly, this lesson is just a brief overview of keeping Jesus Christ at the heart of your marriage. In Christian bookstores or online, you can easily find prayer books, devotional materials, and your church denomination may also have suggestions for your faith walk as a couple. Perhaps together, list ways in which you want to grow in your Christian faith within your home. Again, you need "the LORD to build your home" (see Psalm 127). With almighty God by your side, I believe both of you can strive as a couple for *regular worship, prayer, and devotions.* Your greatest strength and foundation will always be in God alone, so grow together in your faith.

18. PLAN FOR MARITAL SATISFACTION

One word often explains the difference between happy and unhappy couples and that word is PLANNING. In the Bible, God tells us, "The plans of the diligent lead surely to abundance and advantage" (Proverbs 21:5 AMP). Due to a lack of both daily and long-term *marital planning,* dissatisfied and struggling couples let their times together happen by chance. In other words, any positive time together is purely accidental.

Couples who don't plan are destined to collapse relationally and even financially. Hence, due to a lack of planning quality time with one another, far too many couples end up separated or divorced. Happy couples do not ask, "How is our marriage going?" but instead they ask, "What future behavioral plans can we make together in order to enhance our closeness?" Overcome taking each other for granted by always *planning* for a gratifying marriage!

Planning is just a part of life. You plan for vacations. You plan for birthday parties. You plan for major purchases. You plan for Christmas by purchasing gifts, decorating your home, and marking the calendar for get-togethers with friends and family. You may plan for retirement.

Successful businesses plan with definite goals that are written for each department and then regularly reviewed. Salespeople plan by setting goals in order to reach their monthly, quarterly, and yearly quotas. On an individual level, research confirms that successful people have written clearly defined goals—a game plan. Unfortunately, fewer than 5 percent of people write down their individual yearly goals to plan for a successful future. Likewise, very few couples *plan for marital satisfaction.*

When you do not *plan time together,* unintentionally you are planning to be "absent" emotionally and physically from your spouse. Absence does not make your hearts grow warmer, only colder. And you can undoubtedly be "absent" from your spouse even while living in your home. Technology, tasks, projects, outside activities, etc., can distance you emotionally from one another. I understand that for your home to function smoothly, important tasks need to be accomplished. However, don't waste your life and destroy your marriage by doing meaningless tasks or wasting time on projects rather than strengthening your relationship.

One sad example was an unhealthy wife who planned extensively for tasks and projects around their house. During a counseling session, she told her husband, "We just have too many household tasks and projects to complete before we can schedule a *date your mate,* go on a mini-vacation, or do any other fun activity together." Tragically, their hearts grew cold, and their marriage ended in divorce. She now has an enormous amount of time for tasks and projects.

A wonderful synonym for *love* is *time*! You can determine what you love in life by how you spend your time. I want to ask you a few simple marital goal questions: Over the next seven days, have you specifically *planned* for quality time with your spouse? During the next week, on what days do you *plan* to emotionally connect through your *eye-to-eye heart talk*? In terms of creating a stronger bond, have you *planned* for your next two monthly *date your mate* activities outside the home together? How many enrichment minutes will you *plan* to spend together each day during this week? At this moment, do you know what you will do together next weekend? Finally, identify the three most enjoyable things you have done together, and then discuss together when you can *plan* to do those pleasing activities again.

I estimate that less than 5 percent of couples *plan* for time together each day, each week, and each year. I absolutely believe for you to be happy, it is unquestioningly essential that you conscientiously *plan* time together for the upcoming week. Truly the difference between satisfactory relationships and unhappy ones depends on *planning* for emotional attachment time together.

All couples have hectic schedules, but gratifying marriages *plan* for enjoyable activities. Consciously planning and scheduling relationship time makes the critical difference. It takes preparation and time together to stay in love, so take no chances! On a weekly basis, purposefully establish what you can do *daily* to keep your relationship healthy. *Plan* now for you and your spouse to be within the top 5 percent of couples that set goals and *plan* for a rich, rewarding relationship. Love your spouse by making a commitment to *plan* for spending time together during this next week. Marriage is hard work, and success is only achieved through *planning time together for continual growth!*

19. GIVE A DAILY APPRECIATION VITAMIN

The Bible encourages positive words for relationships: "A word aptly spoken is like apples of gold in settings of silver" (Proverbs 25:11 NIV). The apostle Paul also realized the importance of gratitude and appreciation. Hence, he continually praised his fellow believers throughout his thirteen letters in the New Testament. The apostle Paul said, "First, I thank my God through Jesus Christ for all of you" (Romans 1:8 AMP). Paul also declared, "I do not cease to give thanks for you, remembering you in my prayers" (Ephesians 1:16 AMP).

Praise creates positive energy in all relationships, but praise is particularly important for your marriage. When you affirm your spouse, your spouse feels important, significant, and valued. And when both of you feel important, significant, and valued, you feel much more optimistic about your relationship.

Unfortunately, very few spouses offer regular compliments and praise to their partner. With almost every troubled couple that I have ever counseled, *appreciation* or *compliments* were frequently missing aspects. When there is little expression of gratitude and appreciation, complacency takes hold, creating the negative habit of taking each other for granted. Two wonderful gifts of love are gratitude and *appreciation*, or *compliments*!

Definitely, non-loving words spoken to your spouse will tear down your relationship and not build it up. On the other hand, when you focus on being thankful for your spouse's qualities, the little annoyances do not get in the way as much. So, it is so very important to look at the whole marriage in order to search for the "good" in each other rather than just criticizing or complaining about minor flaws. When both you and your spouse commit to searching for positive qualities and actions in each other, your marriage atmosphere will become a more encouraging environment.

You have two choices. You can randomly demonstrate *appreciation* and gratitude, or you can decide to be a cheerleader for your spouse, daily appreciating or praising your partner. Mark Twain said, "I can live for two weeks on one good compliment." A distressed wife told me, "It bums me out because I don't get appreciated by my husband for anything." On the positive side, a wife whose husband began praising and thanking her on a daily basis said to me, "My husband appreciates me so much it has become sweetly sickening, but I love it."

God's Word says, "The tongue has the power of life and death" (Proverbs 18:21 NIV). Words are powerful! Never underestimate the marital strength behind gratitude and appreciation. Nurturing words value your spouse, while lack of appreciation actually devalues your partner. Thus, healthy spouses are "good finders," NOT "fault finders."

Spouses who have an attitude of gratitude are also more optimistic. Optimistic spouses are often healthier physically and usually more satisfied with life. The quality of your marriage can easily be assessed by how frequently you express both gratitude *AND appreciation* for one another. Gratitude and appreciation are not just a reflection of a happy marriage, but both are causes for marital satisfaction.

Gratitude and *appreciation* are different types of affirmation, but both are absolutely essential for a satisfying marriage. Expressing gratitude is a thankful acknowledgment of positive words or actions performed by your spouse. When you express gratitude toward your spouse, you usually use the words "thank you." For example, "Thank you for cleaning up the kitchen," "Thank you for mowing the grass," or "Thank you for cooking dinner." Strive to express gratitude at least once a day.

Appreciation is a form of *praise* or a *compliment*. I call this form of praise the *daily appreciation vitamin*. You may or may not take a daily vitamin for your physical well-being, but both of you certainly need *appreciation vitamins* for your marital well-being. By

way of example, when I say to you, "I appreciate your commitment to reading this book to improve as a spouse," that probably
feels more encouraging and uplifting than when I say, "Thank
you for reading this book in order to improve as a spouse."

The goal for your financial investments and assets is appreciation. Similarly, your goal should be to increase the value of your
spouse's self-worth as well as the value of your relationship. Let
your spouse know what satisfies you with your specific praise. In
addition, the most significant *appreciation* is public praise. When
you *appreciate* your spouse's character qualities in public or during conversations with family and friends, your bond almost certainly becomes unbreakable. What exists in a growing, healthy
relationship is daily *appreciation* that increases your spouse's
self-worth and adds value to your marriage.

One way to evaluate your gratitude and *appreciation* is to place
five coins in your right pocket. Daily, every time you say either
"thank you" or "I *appreciate* you . . . ," move a coin to your left
pocket. However, every time you correct, criticize, or complain
to your spouse, move a coin from the left pocket back to your
right pocket. How many days in a week are you able to move
five coins from your right pocket to your left one? This exercise will speak volumes about your relationship and your marital
satisfaction.

It is such a simple thing, yet it is very important to say to one
another on a daily basis, "I *appreciate* . . ." When you offer regular, specific expressions of appreciation, you will find it much
more difficult to criticize. "I *appreciate* . . ." is one good way of
acknowledging how much you value your spouse. *Keep in mind,
your praise MUST ALWAYS be honest and sincere.* And to improve
your marriage even more, praise particularly those areas where
you desire growth in your spouse. In order to feel valued, perhaps even share with your spouse actions, accomplishments,
words, or tasks you perform about which you desire more compliments and appreciation.

The most powerful form of communication is written. Thus, written notes of *appreciation* are even more special and important than spoken words. These *written appreciation* notes make your spouse feel valued and loved. Plus, these written notes can be saved and reread as a reminder of the love between the two of you.

The key ingredients for a satisfying marriage are *appreciation or praise* and gratitude. Abundant *appreciation* and gratitude are also signs of a loving, committed spouse. Praise and thankfulness are probably the best way to say, "I love you," and there can never be too much love in your marriage. Expressing gratitude for even small actions, coupled with praising your spouse, leads to a healthy relationship for a lifetime. Such positive expressions will warm your hearts, helping both of you work even harder at serving each other. Starting today, never let a day go by without giving an *appreciation vitamin* or thanking your spouse for some action or quality!

20. AIM FOR A MINIMUM OF TWELVE "QUICK CONNECTS" PER DAY

The Bible encourages you to frequently connect with your spouse and states, "Therefore encourage and comfort one another and build up one another, just as you are doing" (1 Thessalonians 5:11 AMP). Today our lives are enhanced because of technological improvements that offer instant gratification. You give your cell phone a five-minute charge before leaving your house, quickly charge an electric razor, hastily warm food in the microwave, and glance at the world news headlines on the Internet. Simply stated, these *quick connections* help life become more enjoyable and convenient. Why not aim to *quickly connect*, or strengthen and build up your partner, too?

We all love attention. A simple way to give your spouse attention and make them feel special is by touching base with them through what I call *quick connects*. A reasonable goal is to have at least *twelve quick connects* per day (six per partner)—this is an easy way to stay emotionally connected, which will definitely heighten your contentment.

I suggest the *spiritual quick connect—prayer, technology quick connects,* and *physical quick connects.* The *spiritual quick connect— prayer* not only fastens your relationship tightly to almighty God, but it also cements your marital connection. Colossians 4:2 encourages, "Be persistent and devoted to prayer" (AMP). The Bible also states, "All these with one mind and one purpose were continually devoting themselves to prayer" (Acts 1:14 AMP). Psalm 88:13 declares, "And in the morning my prayer comes before You" (NKJV). From morning till night, pray together before every meal, pray together over concerns with life, and pray with one another before retiring for the night. Prayer does attach you spiritually and emotionally, and most importantly, prayer strengthens your faith and trust in the One who instituted marriage, our Lord God.

Technology quick connects include text messages, e-mails, and brief phone calls. Text messages can be as brief as abbreviations: "PFY"—praying for you; "TAY"—thinking about you; "LY"—love you; or "MY"—miss you. E-mails can also be concise, but even brief e-mails keep you in touch with one another. In some relationships, due to work schedules, a ten-minute phone call is unrealistic, but a sixty-second call just to say, "I love you" and ask "How is your day going?" is achievable and can help maintain your emotional bond.

One couple told me that their marriage became more satisfying when each of them started sending one text in the morning and one in the afternoon. Another couple said they started e-mailing six or seven times per day and always included the words, "I love you," and this made a big difference in their marital satisfaction. I realize that some spouses have jobs that do not allow for text messages, e-mails, or phone calls. In those situations, the *twelve quick connects* will come from *physical connects* and *prayer*.

The *physical quick connects* are in addition to the *ten-second hug* and the *ten-second kiss*. *Physical quick connects* are pecks—quick kisses, quick hugs, times of hand holding, and just plain physical touches. The power of touch is worth a thousand words. Never neglect the essential ingredient of touch for your marriage. Touch profoundly affects us physically, emotionally, and relationally. *Physical connects* allow us to communicate our love without even saying a word. While partners may have differing ideas about what touch feels the best, satisfied couples have spouses who touch each other frequently. A great question to ask your spouse is, "What types of simple touches are especially meaningful for you?"

Without *twelve quick connects* every day, stress and tension are more likely to be present. During a session, I once shared with one husband the importance of connecting daily. He immediately said, "I think we will find it very difficult to do even four *quick connects* per day." At the next session, both spouses reported a "strong disconnect and extreme tension," and the husband was correct—they rarely achieved even four *quick connects* a day.

On the positive side, one wife told me, "I think we can attain thirty *quick connects* per day." At the next session, the wife reported that she and her husband easily surpassed twelve *quick connects*, averaging more than twenty *quick connects* per day. How would you assess that couple's emotional union, as well as the stress between them? You are right! Tension was low, and both reported consistent marital happiness.

To always connect via technology, without an additional mixture of prayer and physical connects, will not solidify your bond as strongly as you both desire. Whenever possible, attempt to demonstrate a balanced mixture of *prayer, technology,* and *physical quick connects* to strengthen your love.

In the beginning, one way to focus regularly on *quick connects* is to set a goal to treat each other similarly to your dating days, like a girlfriend and a boyfriend would treat each other. Ask yourself this key question: "Today, will I be a boyfriend or girlfriend to my spouse?" If the answer is yes, you probably will also do a minimum of *twelve quick connects*. Daily, when you choose to connect with your partner, you automatically are focused on keeping your spouse as your number-one priority. These three connections act like super glue for your relationship.

21. TRY QUIET CONNECTS

Almighty God tells us in Psalm 46:10: "Be still and know (recognize, understand) that I am God" (AMP). One challenge for most of us is to be still and silent or quiet. For your marriage, silence is truly golden when it comes to technology. Simply stated, technology is not real life. Technology can be truly ugly because your bonding times together are often diminished when technology is on. Thus, set a goal to have quiet connects. *Quiet connects* are a "noise fast," and an essential goal that can occur either at home or in the car.

Recently, hundreds of houses in our hometown lost power for a couple of days due to a storm. One couple I counseled shared with me that the loss of power was a huge blessing for their marriage. With the power out, this couple brought out the candles and described their evening as completely restorative and peaceful. With absolutely no distractions and nothing to do but talk and touch, their emotional closeness grew, and both agreed that it was "one of the best nights ever in our marriage." This couple also set a goal to turn off technology every night for a period of time.

I cannot count the numerous couples that have experienced heartache in their relationship due to some type of "technology addiction." Ask yourself two questions: "How much time do I spend with technology versus how much time do I spend with my spouse?" And: "How much time do I actually spend with technology in twenty-four hours?" I am asking you to evaluate all technology, not just television and your computer, but also cell phones, notebooks, portable music players, handheld games, etc.

The absolute truth is that couples satisfied with their marital happiness are usually intentional with *quiet connects*. Quiet time together leads to closeness for your relationship! Begin with small amounts of time, and watch your relationship grow by turning off ALL technology during this time. Perhaps even have NO technology one day per week. At times, when riding in the car together, turn off the radio and use that time to connect with each other. You will be amazed how emotionally bonded you can become by planning for that *positive quiet time* of sharing feelings, thoughts, dreams, and ideas with one another.

22. FOUR DAILY ESSENTIALS

In 1 Corinthians 13:4 we read, "Love endures with patience and serenity, love is kind and thoughtful" (AMP). Spouses who are kind and thoughtful daily prove their love by sharing those magical words: "I love you."

Couples with satisfying relationships possess *four daily essentials*. I label the first two the *two goods*, which are: *"Good-bye, I love you,"* and *"Good night, I love you."* The third essential is the *first five minutes* together each day. The fourth essential is *two within twenty*, meaning connect for just *two minutes within the first twenty minutes* when you see each other at the conclusion of the day. Every year I have to earn twenty hours of continuing education to keep my counseling license. Likewise, the *four daily essentials* help you earn your partner's love every single day of your marriage.

It happens so subtly and yet it is so insidious when the three words *I love you* begin to disappear from a marriage relationship.

One dissatisfied wife said, "My husband's family was non-affectionate and nonverbal, and he also rarely initiates an 'I love you'." Sadly, one wife actually shared her untrue perception: "I don't have to say I love you because I say those words by the things I do." I have seen spouses in pain simply because those words were infrequently spoken or even never spoken.

Remember, before marriage, you probably told each other over and over "*I love you.*" You felt important, worthwhile, and valued. You felt validated that you were the number-one priority with those words, "*I love you.*" When both of you initiate saying, "*I love you,*" it strengthens your "oneness." Frequently using the words "*I love you*" keeps your marriage fresh and alive.

Often, an accurate barometer for your marriage can be gauged by how often you proclaim those powerful words, "*I love you.*" Ask yourself right now, "How often do I take the initiative with those three magical words, *I love you*?" To remain in love, both of you need to use those simple yet powerful words. And when possible look into each other's eyes when you say them.

First Essential "Good": Whenever either one of you leaves the house, the one leaving should always initiate a "*Good-bye, I love you.*" A practical rhyme can help, "I will never leave our house without kissing and hugging my spouse," and then add, "*Good-bye, I love you.*"

Second Essential "Good": Whoever goes to bed first always initiates a "*Good night, I love you.*" In another chapter, I share important ideas about sleep, but for now it is very essential to go to sleep on a positive note. Going to sleep with the words "*Good night, I love you*" ringing in your ears may also help you achieve a restful night's sleep.

One spouse told me, "My partner almost never says the words *I love you* **first**." The *two goods* will help overcome that problem. Thus, never leave your home or go to bed without creating a positive memory by giving a kiss, hug, and sharing those three unifying words, *I love you*. By implementing the *two goods*, you will at least say the three special words a minimum of two times each day.

Third Essential—First Five Minutes: What is it like to begin the day in your home? Each morning set a positive atmosphere for your relationship by being kind and pleasant, not grumpy. I am not suggesting that you have to be bubbly and giddy with joy. And you may not feel like being overly nurturing, but please don't be critical, complaining, or condemning. Beginning the *first five minutes* of your day on a constructive note establishes a healthy emotional connection. Start the day with positive, considerate interaction—physical touches, supportive words, and healthy behaviors—cultivating a good attitude with your spouse and marriage. When the *first five minutes* of contact with your spouse is positive, it is highly probable that the remainder of your day will be constructive, as well.

Fourth Essential—Two Minutes Within Twenty Minutes: What feelings do you have when you think about coming home after work? Do you look forward to reconnecting as a couple, or do you have an apprehensive feeling? Although it is not the same for every healthy couple, hopefully you acknowledge your spouse with a smile and a warm "hi" with focused eye contact, and then a quick kiss. After coming back together, such a warm welcome reunites your commitment for a satisfying relationship. A brief, positive rebonding is important, but the next step of planning for *two special minutes within twenty minutes* is just as essential.

Please do not demand or even expect that the *two minutes* happen immediately when arriving home. Over the years, hundreds of spouses have told me that they almost feel "attacked" with information when coming home at the end of the day. Usually, when one of you is immediately pounced on by the other partner, the result will be a tense, unpleasant evening.

After a quick, positive reentry routine, allow the spouse who just arrived some time to unwind and briefly relax. Permit a change of clothes, a shower, a glance at the newspaper, a peek at the mail, etc. After that transitory recharge time, find a few minutes for warming your hearts by looking into each other's eyes, attentively listening to your spouse, and showing an interest. However, this is not a time to "dump" frustrations, discuss problems to be resolved, or rehash terrible moments throughout the day. This is a time for *two minutes* of emotional intimacy. Perhaps ask each other about happy moments that day. During this time, also give each other a *meaningful kiss* and *hug*.

By always spending a vital *two minutes within the first twenty minutes*, you can daily restore your emotional bond. *Two positive minutes* will almost guarantee an encouraging atmosphere for the remainder of your evening.

In conclusion, what are the *four daily essentials*?

1. *"Good-bye, I love you."*
2. *"Good night, I love you."*
3. Positive *first five minutes* in the morning,
4. Connect for *two minutes within the first twenty minutes* at the conclusion of the day.

23. MEALTIMES ARE SIGNIFICANT OCCASIONS FOR YOUR MARRIAGE

In biblical times, meals at a table were integral in building relationships and sharing life together. Acts 2:46 encourages, "Day after day they met in the temple [area] continuing with one mind, and breaking bread in various private homes. They were eating their meals together with joy and generous hearts" (AMP). Every couple needs to follow the example of the early Christians when it comes to meals together.

I am both amazed and saddened at how many couples do not have regular meals together. A common denominator for many troubled marriages is a lack of *mealtimes together*. Too often I have heard comments like, "We eat dinner at different times," "We both fend for ourselves," and "My spouse refuses to cook."

I could provide numerous examples of unhappy, troubled couples not eating together. One husband made a plate of whatever he could find and then ate in the bedroom. Another wife fixed her plate and stood at the kitchen island by herself. Many couples have told me they eat in front of the television and say absolutely nothing while eating their meal. One husband even said, "My wife and I know we should not eat in front of the television, but we do it anyway." Hurting spouses do not realize that *mealtimes are significant occasions for emotionally bonding their hearts.*

Due to work schedules, I understand that a realistic number of meals together may vary from couple to couple. Nonetheless when you are home together, definitely plan each mealtime to be with each other at a table. Whether you are having a hot meal or just sandwiches and chips, I strongly urge you to sit at the kitchen or dining room table with absolutely no distractions—the television off, no form of technology, and no newspaper, magazine, or book.

At *mealtimes*, only accentuate the positive! Never discuss any problems from work, negative issues with the family, expenses with the home, or any other life difficulties. Talk about what brought you joy during the day or perhaps blessings that happened for which you are grateful.

Once you begin *making meals a regular bonding time*, you will be amazed at the improved connection with one another. You will not only be closer emotionally as a couple, but there will also be less tension. Again, remember Lesson 18, that satisfied, happy couples *plan time together*, including *mealtimes*.

24. GO OVERBOARD ON POLITENESS

The Bible reminds us, "Whoever sows sparingly will also reap sparingly, and whoever sows generously will also reap generously" (2 Corinthians 9:6 NIV). When two spouses abundantly sow politeness, then they will also reap civility, respect, and courteous manners.

I have never seen one struggling couple where *politeness* reigned supreme in their relationship. With troubled marriages, snarky, impolite comments usually dominate daily interaction. By being extra-*polite* with each other, you add a higher level of respect to your relationship, besides a profound degree of emotional closeness. Being extra-considerate on a daily basis fosters a gracious spirit, leading to a rewarding marriage. Never underestimate the power of your words!

During your dating days, both of you were probably extra-courteous using those well-mannered words: "please," "thank you," and "you're welcome." For whatever reason, in a struggling marriage, being gracious and nice becomes a distant reality.

An adulterous spouse once told me, "The affair partner was not particularly attractive but was extra-nice, paid me numerous compliments, gave me attention, and through their kindness made me feel very important." I am not excusing the sin of adultery, but just helping you understand that politeness is like a magnet.

An unhealthy husband told his wife, "If you think I need to use 'please,' 'thank you,' and 'you're welcome,' then you are being overly sensitive." Most of his other relationships also lacked civility. This husband also had almost no friends, as well as minimal connections with family members. Sadly, I was unable to convince him that the common courtesy of *polite words* was important for all his relationships, and his marriage ended in divorce.

Daily demonstrate at least *one polite behavior* or courteous phrase to enrich your marriage. Definitely being extra-polite and kind lowers the stress and tension in your relationship. Avoid letting a day pass where you do not use *"PLEASE," "THANK YOU,"* and *"YOU'RE WELCOME"* with your spouse. When both of you use those *three courtesies* every day, then you increase the odds for a rich, rewarding relationship.

25. LAUGH TOGETHER

A simple barometer for determining your emotional health is your sense of humor. For years, *laughter* has been known to be the "good medicine" for maintaining your physical and emotional health. Best of all, laughter is free! *Laughter* releases your pent-up frustrations and is a wonderful stress relief for both your life and your marital relationship. Healthy individuals can laugh at themselves, at their marital "fumbles," and even at life circumstances beyond their control.

How important is *laughter* for your marriage? Proverbs 17:22 states, "A joyful heart is good medicine, but a crushed spirit dries up the bones (ESV)." Ecclesiastes 3:4 reminds us that there is "a time to weep and a time to laugh" (NIV). *Laughing together* actually helps with the emotion of love in marriage, and without it there is a void. A widow who was married over fifty years said, "I tell every couple I know, enjoy your time together, and the best way to do that is to daily laugh together." Another woman widowed twice said, "If I could suggest one piece of advice to any single person looking for a spouse, it is to search for a partner with a sense of humor. A sense of humor coupled with laughter makes everything in life not so serious and stressful." Both widows are absolutely correct!

A marriage without *laughter* has no sparkle. It is difficult to have joy and happiness in a marriage when the two of you rarely laugh together. To have a healthy marriage, you must be able to jointly *laugh* at life, mistakes, silly stuff, etc.—but never at each other!

Having a successful marriage is difficult without simple laughter and positive humor. Daily life and marital irritations can easily frustrate you, but *laughter* can be one of the healing balms that helps overcome those common annoyances. Humor and *laughter* are often one of the greatest solutions for marital struggles. Frequently talk about the funniest occurrences that have happened in life, at work, in your relationships, etc.

In addition, greet your spouse with a *smile*, not a frown. Smile a lot at each other. One spouse said, "When my sweetheart gives me her million-dollar smile, I feel especially valued." Smiling not only positively impacts the chemicals within your brain, but it also has a constructive effect on your relationship. Frequently wearing a *smile* around your home creates a relaxed atmosphere. And a *smile* gives your spouse a reason to emotionally connect with you.

Always avoid using belittling humor with each other. Belittling humor creates a wall between the two of you. So, remember to laugh *WITH* your spouse and *never AT* them. Laughing at your spouse's expense is demeaning and hurts your relationship. In addition, avoid being around negative, cynical individuals who drain your "laughing spirit." Instead, associate with positive, hopeful, fun-loving, and joyful individuals. Being around happy people will actually help you practice your smile and laugh.

I realize that some people grew up in a home without observing *laughter* and a sense of humor. If you are one of those individuals, you may find it challenging to frequently smile, display simple laughter, and manifest positive humor. If laughter does not come naturally, you may need to practice daily developing your sense of humor. Perhaps watch comedy television shows or movies, but please do whatever it takes to develop your sense of humor and thus create a lighthearted atmosphere within your home. A sense of humor is contagious and spreads cheerfulness throughout your relationship.

Laughter, humor, and a smile definitely matter! A daily smile and a hearty laugh are indispensable for the tensions of life, as well as for your relationship. *Laughing together*, coupled with a sense of humor, is almost required for handling the challenges of married life. When you are enjoying married life together, you will also be *laughing together*. Daily set a goal of smiling at your spouse several times and note the difference in your emotional connection. For your marriage, the formula is: Two merry hearts equal one satisfying relationship. A marriage full of smiles, *laughter*, and humor can be a rich blessing that leads to lifelong happiness.

26. TELL YOUR SPOUSE HOW TO COMFORT YOU

Throughout the Bible, God provides words of *comfort*, and He expects us to do likewise. We are told in 2 Corinthians 1:3-4, "Blessed [gratefully praised and adored] be the God and Father of our Lord Jesus Christ, the Father of mercies and the God of all comfort, who comforts and encourages us in every trouble so that we will be able to comfort and encourage those who are in any kind of trouble, with the comfort with which we ourselves are comforted by God" (AMP). *Comfort* is a significant attribute for every Christian spouse to possess.

Frequently when counseling couples, I hear spouses complain, "My spouse doesn't know how to comfort me when I am going through a tough time." Yet when I ask them to share five phrases they would like to hear, or five actions their spouse could demonstrate to lift their low emotions or comfort them, the answer is "I don't know. They should just know how to console me." In my counseling experience, I never had even one spouse initially suggest five phrases or five actions that would help them feel better.

Reflect back on your past life trials and what people said to you or did for you that helped you handle those challenges. I encourage you to also return to your childhood and ask this essential question: "How did my mother, father, grandmother, or grandfather comfort me as a child when I had a painful problem?" Over 90 percent of spouses have told me, "I really can't ever remember being comforted by my parents or grandparents or stepparents." Hence, based on your experiences with significant others, you may find it a challenge to identify what *comforting* words or actions you would like from your spouse.

Everyone can have discouraging days, weeks, or even months. When you are in a low mood, what you seek from your spouse is compassion and consolation. Yet no one can read minds, and very often we expect our spouses to do just that. So, if you don't know how you desire to be comforted, how can your spouse possibly know? In addition, the specific words and actions you desire for comfort may be totally different from what your spouse desires when they need to be soothed.

To cope with difficult life stressors, I encourage you to personally answer two questions: First, do you know specifically how you want to be *comforted* when you go through a low mood or various trials of life? Second, have you precisely told your spouse what they can *DO* or *SAY* to help? Like almost every spouse I have posed these questions to, your answer is probably "no."

When you are feeling down, your spouse can only help if they know what lifts your spirits. Sometime soon, will you please sit in your living room or at the kitchen table and share with each other your thoughts and feelings about what will bring comfort to you in stressful situations? During that conversation, begin showing compassion for your partner by echoing back your spouse's suggestions for comfort and ask, "Is that correct?"

Next, I encourage both of you to complete the following *comfort activity*. Individually, write down a minimum of five *phrases* that you want to hear when you are going through tough times.

Some spouses have included statements like, "I love you no matter what"; "You are special to me"; "With God's help, you can cope"; "I am praying for you"; "I care deeply about you"; "Let's sit down and pray together"; or "I know you will overcome this challenge." You can use these statements or come up with five different phrases that will bring you *comfort*.

In addition, please write down at least five *actions* your partner could take that would provide you some *comfort*. Keep in mind that these actions need to be small, achievable goals. I had one spouse once request the time-consuming activity of "Bake me a cherry pie," which of course would bring most of us comfort, but is also a major project.

For action examples, some spouses have written down: "Hold my hand for five minutes"; "Sit on the sofa next to me and watch a thirty-minute television show together"; "Give me a ten-second neck massage"; "Give me a two-minute foot massage"; Bring me a cup of coffee"; or "Go for a five-minute walk with me around our neighborhood."

Once you both have your written answers, exchange papers and place them in your top dresser drawer or some other accessible location. Then, when your spouse is feeling low, pick one phrase you can say and one action you can do from their *comfort activity* list to lift their mood. The *comfort activity* is essential for your marriage because demonstrating compassion and kindness toward your spouse when they are low will not only benefit your spouse, but it will also emotionally connect the two of you.

27. SAFEGUARD SLEEP

For both of you, getting enough *sleep* is an extremely important goal! Psalm 127:2 states, "It is vain for you to rise early, to retire late, to eat the bread of anxious labors—for He gives [blessings] to His beloved even in his sleep" (AMP). Before marriage, you probably looked forward to *sleeping together* nightly for your entire life. It is truly a joy and privilege to *sleep together* in the same bed. And by physically sleeping in the same bed, you bind yourselves emotionally together just due to physical proximity alone.

I am amazed at how often I see couples for an initial assessment and their main problem is sleep issues. Staying up late at night or having an unstructured sleep schedule makes a person prone to anxiety, eating problems, depression, disorganization, irresponsible actions, and even mental illness. Sleep deprivation often leads to fatigue, creating irritability, thus producing major arguments in a marriage.

I have seen too many couples have troubled marriages due to one or both spouses having unhealthy sleep habits. *DANGER!* Sleeping in bed alone leads to emotional distance between the two of you. Not sleeping in the same bed may also create sexual intimacy problems, with a negative spiral toward severe unhappiness. Never punish your spouse by not sleeping with them because that is destructive. Another warning: When you have dogs or cats or even children in bed, that builds a "wall" between the two of you.

I understand that some spouses have sleep apnea, toss and turn, snore, etc., making it difficult to sleep in the same bed. Nonetheless, when you sleep in different locations, you have more of a partnership than a marriage. So always seek solutions to any issues that do not allow for physical closeness throughout the night. Wear earplugs, wear a sleep mask, invest in a white noise machine, do whatever it takes for the "physical oneness" of sleep time.

One wife said, "When Sam does not work, he does not go to bed until 2:00 a.m. By staying up late, he doesn't allow for us to have cuddle time. And he is more likely to be easily agitated and irritated the next day. His self-esteem is also lowered because late at night he munches on food, thus gaining weight, feeling even worse about himself, and now he is depressed." I am extremely happy to share that when this woman's husband developed healthy sleep habits, their marriage improved immensely.

Please realize that sleeping in bed together is a sign of commitment and love that essentially unites the two of you, even while you sleep. However, if you are unable to sleep together, agree to snuggle for even a couple of minutes before going to your own beds. Cuddling in bed, perhaps in the nude, a few times a week for several minutes with or without any sexual contact affirms your love for each other.

When you have sound *sleep habits*, you will often also have a byproduct of healthier sexual intimacy. Two wholesome spouses go to bed together about the same time every night. Weekends are the exception, since many people may not work on Saturday and Sunday and like to relax a little later into the evening. I encourage you and your spouse to develop two sleep goals. First, sleep in the same bed, and second, try to go to sleep at about the same time every night. Whatever you decide, develop *sleep safeguards* to protect your relationship.

28. NURTURE THROUGH NAMES

Names are deeply important in the Bible. Adam comes from the Hebrew word "ground," meaning he was "formed from the dust of the ground." Jesus has more than forty names in the Bible, and all of them have special significance. Just a few examples: the name Jesus means "Savior" because Jesus saves; "Immanuel" means "God with us"; Christ means "Anointed One," and in the Hebrew it is the equivalent of "Messiah."

So, it makes perfect sense that *names* will be equally essential for producing a satisfying marriage. One major goal for your marriage is to value each other in order to achieve emotional oneness, and a vital way to achieve that objective is through *names*. Words are like food, so nurture each other with *wholesome healthy names*.

If you have children, when they are present it is okay to call each other "mom" and "dad." But when the children are *not* present, DO NOT call each other "mom" and "dad." I once heard a seventy-five-year old wife refer to her husband as "daddy" even when they were with other adults.

First names, positive names, or *pet names* are healthy for your marital relationship and generate a necessary intimate union. Hearing your spouse call your *name* or endearing you with *nurturing names* creates a feeling of love. Be extra-sweet with your *pet names.* Some examples are: angel, honey, doll, sweetheart, cutie, sexy, handsome, beautiful, lover boy, babe, sweet pea, hunk, goddess, peaches, gorgeous, sweetie, precious, good-looking, sugar, darling, stud, etc.

Using sincere *pet names* is well worth your effort because your spouse will begin to fulfill the name or label you give them. *Pet names* create a kind of secret language between the two of you. And using *pet names* automatically increases your marital romance and heightens your emotional connection.

29. GIFTS DEMONSTRATE CARE

"The free gift of God [that is, His remarkable, overwhelming gift of grace to believers] is eternal life in Christ Jesus our Lord" (Romans 6:23 AMP). 2 Corinthians 9:15 reminds us to give "thanks ... to God for His indescribable gift" (AMP). Truly, eternal life in heaven is God's gift to us simply through faith in Jesus Christ, the Son of God. Our Creator gives us a special gift; doesn't it then make sense to regularly give *gifts* to our spouse?

Hence, one way to show you genuinely care and appreciate your spouse is through *gifts.* Those *gifts* may be inexpensive or even free, but they signify that you truly value your partner. One significant way to demonstrate love comes from giving *gifts.* On the flip side, in struggling marriages, gifts and cards have usually been absent for years.

Use your imagination in giving *gifts* and win your spouse's heart over and over again. Treating your spouse with gifts helps them feel valued, special, and important in your eyes, and that creates love within your partner. Every little *gift* means a lot! The amount of the gift is not as important as the fact that you are thinking of ways to make your partner feel wanted and needed.

For example, I counseled a wife who gave daily gifts to her husband that cost less than $1 for thirty consecutive days before his birthday. This wife had deep respect for her husband and wanted him to understand how special and wonderful he was to her. Her simple idea led her husband to respond with even more tenderness, kindness, and nurture for his wife.

Always remember your spouse's birthday, Valentine's Day, and your anniversary. *Gifts* and cards for special occasions do cost money, but the effort and time keeps the two of you emotionally connected. Perhaps consider making your own card, which is also a gift of your time. Through *gifts* and cards, you demonstrate that your spouse is number one in your life because you willingly took the time to make them feel extraordinary.

30. TAKE REGULAR MINI-VACATIONS

Genesis 2:2 states, "He rested on the seventh day from all His work that he had done" (ESV) If almighty God took a break after Creation, it only makes sense that couples need "breaks" or "mini-vacations," as well.

If you rate your marriage with a B- or higher, there is a significant probability you take regular *mini-vacations*. My definition of a *mini-vacation* is being away from your home for one or two nights, preferably in another town or city. Although I suggest four *mini-vacations* each year, I realize that is often unattainable due to finances, work responsibilities, children, family commitments, etc. However, a simple change of environment can often recharge your relationship.

A key question to ask yourself is, "When was the last time we went to a hotel for one or two nights for a mini-vacation?" Some spouses will complain about the money spent for a mini-vacation. Yet, two mini-vacations costing $150 each, for a total of $300, is the approximate hourly cost for most divorce lawyers in the city where I live. I think that $300 per year for two mini-vacations is a much better investment than thousands of dollars in divorce legal fees.

Mini-vacations are necessities, not luxuries. A special getaway permits you to concentrate entirely on each other. Start today to plan for one-on-one time away from home to enhance your marital relationship. Initially, you may only have a *mini-vacation* once per year but that is at least a start. Or if you can go on two *mini-vacations* per year, then each of you should choose one.

Begin by fantasizing what both of you believe would be a wonderful *mini-vacation*. Independently write down your top five mini-vacations. Then together narrow the list and agree on your top five. Next, decide together when and where you will have your first mini-vacation. Whoever does not select the first mini-vacation will choose the next one and then continue alternating future mini-vacations.

For your first *mini-vacation*, I suggest leaving on a Friday or Saturday afternoon so that you can check into the hotel, have dinner, spend the evening together, and return the following day. I realize that money may be an issue for most couples, so let me give you an example of one couple's inexpensive mini-vacation.

First, they chose a hotel in another city with an indoor pool, hot tub, and free continental breakfast. After lunch on a Friday, they traveled to their mini-vacation destination, arriving around 2:00 pm. During the afternoon they lounged around the pool, relaxed in the hot tub, and enjoyed time together without discussing any life issues. This couple packed sandwiches, chips, dessert, and drinks so they could eat dinner at no cost. The couple relaxed and enjoyed their "free" dinner around the pool.

Then, later that evening they went to an inexpensive movie theater. On Saturday morning, they shared how much fun they had just sleeping in, relaxing, and cuddling in bed. After "romantic cuddling," they had a complimentary breakfast together, left the hotel at 10:00 a.m., and arrived home by Saturday noon. The entire cost of their mini-vacation was about $135, including gas. They spent time together from Friday noon through Saturday, and it turned out to be a wonderful weekend.

Hope is so important for your emotional well-being, as well as for your marital happiness. Looking forward to a *mini-vacation* provides hope for the future, so begin planning today for a mini-vacation in the next two to six months. With *mini-vacations*, the possibilities are endless, and the outcome is extremely enjoyable!

31. EVEN-ODD MARRIAGE ENHANCER

Ecclesiastes 3 tells us there is a "time for everything," including a time not to discuss life and relationship issues. Challenges are a regular part of life. I believe that every two months you need to expect a minor crisis—a new washer must be purchased, the brakes on the car need to be replaced, a family member has a health issue, etc.

Words create our life! Too many couples are unhappy because every single day there is complaining and criticizing about life issues for which there are often no solutions. Such negative talk only produces a pessimistic view of life and can even damage your marriage. Daily "problem speech" easily produces a day-after-day downer and may make coming home a miserable experience to be dreaded.

When either one of you experiences a life stressor, implement the *even-odd marriage enhancer*. When I think of the word "even," I think of the words smooth, calm, flat, and tranquil. Thus, on even dates, neither of you can discuss troubling issues or any problem areas of life. On even dates, you can only discuss positives or blessings occurring in your life. The result is that every other day you will be focusing on "happy moments" and not stressful concerns. Hence, 50 percent of your life will be positive.

When I think of the word "odd," I think of out-of-the-ordinary, unique, different, and an unusual occurrence. On odd dates, you may discuss a particular life difficulty or any heartache distressing you emotionally, physically, or relationally. However, you can only have a problem discussion for thirty minutes, and if absolutely necessary, a maximum of sixty minutes. On an odd date, you are limiting negativity in order to enjoy the remainder of both your personal day as well as time with your spouse.

Some couples decide to use the *even-odd marriage enhancer* on a regular basis, not just when they have a life crisis. After utilizing the *even-odd marriage enhancer*, many spouses shared that they did not realize how frequently they complained about their physical ailments and life problems.

Almost 100 percent of couples report a more satisfying relationship when using this excellent tool, the *even-odd marriage enhancer*. In addition, spouses often report being healthier physically because there is certainly a mind-body effect. I have also found that the *even-odd marriage enhancer* significantly improves your perspective regarding your spouse. Finally, the *even-odd marriage enhancer* will probably help both of you develop a more optimistic outlook on life and the future of your marriage.

32. BASIC ESSENTIALS FOR SEXUAL INTIMACY

Sexual intimacy is truly God's precious gift for marriage. Many books have been written about God's gift of sex, so the next three lessons are simply a *brief overview* to improve your physical, sexual, and emotional connection.

The Bible provides three reasons for marriage: companionship, *sexual intimacy*, and children. Having only companionship produces really just a "business partnership," not a "one-flesh union" between husband and wife. In the Old Testament, the term for sexual intercourse was "to know." When a husband and wife are joined together through intercourse, they "know each other" at deeper levels, which is necessary for a gratifying marriage.

Proverbs 5:18–19 encourages a husband, "May your wife be a fountain of blessing for you. Rejoice in the wife of your youth. She is a loving deer, a graceful doe. Let her breasts satisfy you always. May you always be captivated by her love" (NLT). Certainly, these verses apply equally for the wife as well. In 1 Corinthians 7:3, God's Word urges husbands and wives to satisfy each other's sexual needs.

Sexual intimacy and the marriage cannot be placed in two different compartments. Sexual intimacy and the marriage are very much interconnected for relationship satisfaction. Sexual intimacy is not just for physical pleasure, but more importantly it is a way of demonstrating care and affection. Sexual intercourse is a significant way of expressing love for each other and physically saying, "I love you." I understand that physical touch and intercourse are very pleasurable, but more importantly, *sexual intimacy* keeps a couple emotionally bonded and joined in a special "one-flesh union."

When sexual dissatisfaction is present, rarely is there a strong emotional connection. And when there is little sexual intimacy, then you are also more likely to divorce, because one of you is usually very unhappy. One husband said, "We have not had sex in years, and now we live on different floors in our home." A wife told me through her tears, "If my husband only wants to be my 'brother,' that is fine, but I am upset about being only one step better than a sister and I don't want to be married." A husband said, "I try not to even think about sex, but that makes temptation overwhelming." Another wife said, "My husband will not even touch me, and we have not had intercourse in years. Why be married?" A husband shared his troubled feelings: "I am a married priest to my wife and celibate." A wife said, "I was surprised when he moved out of our home," but she went on to report that they had not had sexual intimacy for six months.

Healthy *sexual intimacy* does not necessarily make a satisfying relationship, but it certainly helps with your emotional and physical fulfillment. On the other hand, without regular sexual intimacy, or at a minimum, nude physical closeness, achieving marital satisfaction for both of you may be a challenge. Whatever the reason, a sexless marriage is like a stick of dynamite waiting to explode, because at least one of you will probably be both emotionally and physically depleted.

Half the time, sexual problems are simply due to an unhappy marriage outside the bedroom. However, the other 50 percent of the time stems from one spouse having personal issues. Some of those individual difficulties include inhibitions, anxiety, control issues, past trauma, phobias, eating disorders, etc. Sadly, a spouse with personal issues usually lacks insight, makes constant excuses, and places blame on the other partner for the lack of sexual intimacy within the relationship.

At times, a negative cycle may begin to create serious sexual intimacy difficulties. An example of a negative cycle could include the following: the wife rejects the husband's sexual wishes; the husband gets frustrated and becomes nonattentive; the wife develops an even weaker sex drive; the husband withdraws and becomes even more distant; and that leads to even more infrequent sexual intimacy. Certainly, the cycle could also begin with the husband rejecting the wife's sexual wishes, causing the wife to withdraw from her husband, etc. No matter who starts the negative cycle, the outcome is severe damage to the marriage.

Always remember that compliments, hugs, and kisses at nonsexual times, meaning outside the bedroom, can lead to more fulfilling sexual intimacy later. Especially for a wife, *time together*, *talking together*, and *touching together* outside the bedroom are the very best foreplay. Generally speaking, if I want to know how good a couple's sex life is, all I have to ask are three questions: "How frequently do you physically touch each other?"; "Do both of you initiate physical touch?"; and "How frequently do you converse eye-to-eye with each other?" Lessons 13, 14, and 15 of this book are vital for a rewarding sexual relationship.

Talking outside the bedroom is an unequivocal essential step for your *sexual intimacy*. Strive for warm communication and tender talk to stimulate your emotional connection. For some wives, talking is actually a turn-on. Thus, most wives usually need verbal intercourse before physical intercourse. Particularly for wives, an emotional connection through talking together must happen before the physical connection of sexual intimacy occurs.

Too many spouses fail to also recognize that the nose is sensitive to odors. To have a pleasurable experience, an attractive smell is so very important. I have heard numerous times, "I don't want to be intimate because of bad breath, body odor, or my spouse hasn't showered for more than twenty-four hours and now wants to make love." For good personal hygiene, showering or bathing daily is important, but that is also significant for your relationship as well as your sexual intimacy.

The word "sex" for most wives is a cold word and a turn-off. Having "sex" versus "making love" are two different concepts in a wife's mind. For husbands, instead of requesting "sex," will you please ask your wife to "be romantic"; "make love"; "romantically cuddle"; "be physically intimate"; "be close"; etc.? When a husband avoids the cold word "sex" by lovingly and tenderly requesting sexual intimacy, he can create a strong emotional and sexual bond for his wife by helping her feel valued and special. Remember, a wife must feel valued and cherished before she wants to be sexually intimate. For a husband, sex helps him feel loved and respected.

If either of you was raised by strict parents, where the expectation was to not make any mistakes at home or at school, or where "sex" was a huge taboo, it can become a block to sexual enjoyment. Such a stringent environment may produce adult anxiety, creating a tense feeling where it is difficult to let go and fully enjoy any form of pleasure, sexual or otherwise. I have had spouses say something like, "I never really got in trouble the first eighteen years of my life because I was expected to be perfect by my parents, and now I have the feeling that sex is bad and it is wrong to enjoy sexual intimacy. So, I am uptight in the bedroom, thinking I am doing something immoral."

Don't risk being misunderstood by not specifically requesting sexual intimacy. Whether it is sexual intimacy or any area of your relationship, direct requests with your wants and needs can make your relationship and closeness even more gratifying. Always let your spouse know what brings you the greatest sexual joy. Being specific about what you want in order to be sexually fulfilled also enhances your overall communication skills as a couple. So communicate what you enjoy with such phrases as, "I like. . . "; "It really turns me on when you . . . "; "I love it when you . . ."; and "It feels really good when you . . ."

If there are sexual problems or one of you has a lack of sexual desire, remain hopeful, because both of you working together can definitely improve your sexual intimacy. Please consider the following suggestions:

1. Have a complete physical exam with blood work.
2. Ask your physician about the medications that you take, because some prescribed drugs may numb your sexual desire.
3. Discuss with your spouse how nudity and the topic of sex were handled in your family of origin.
4. With a pastor or counselor, work through any barriers or personal problems like sexual abuse, rape, past promiscuous behavior that creates guilt, etc., that may be preventing you from fully enjoying God's gift of sex.

5. For husbands, consider a testosterone medication or even an erectile dysfunction medication.

In addition, ask key self-evaluation questions:
1. Are you anxious and depressed, because a tense, deflated mood can create emotional paralysis producing a "do-nothing mentality" in most areas of life, including sexual intimacy?
2. Are you eating well-balanced meals?
3. How often are you engaging in even mild exercise?
4. If you are overweight, have the extra pounds created feelings of low self-esteem that are hurting your desire for sexual closeness?
5. What did you intentionally do to attract your spouse when you were dating, and what are you doing now?

Together, discuss these ideas and questions, because your responses may assist both of you in having your physical affection and sexual needs met. Again, numerous Christian books have been written on God's gift of sex, so if you need more sexual intimacy education than what is included in these brief lessons, I encourage you to read a Christian book on sexual intimacy together.

Although sexual fulfillment may be different for each of you, satisfied couples regularly enjoy some form of sexual pleasure in varying degrees. The goal for these *three sexual intimacy lessons* is to provide some basics for establishing fun, playfulness, and togetherness in order to enhance your sexual enjoyment. Remember, a wife needs to feel good about the entire marital relationship in order for *sexual intimacy* to even be considered, while a husband needs *sexual intimacy* to feel admired and respected. For a happy marriage, gratifying sexual expression is an essential part, because it is vital for enhancing your emotional connection.

33. GIVE TWELVE TO TWENTY-FOUR HOURS ADVANCE NOTICE

It has been said that women are Crock-Pots and men are micro-waves, and this is especially true after the age of forty. Like a Crock-Pot, women need to warm up to the idea of sexual intima-cy, fantasize, and move toward the enjoyment of being physically close. Just the opposite, a husband might not have even thought about sexual intimacy before bedtime, but he can watch his wife change into her nightgown, which turns on his microwave for sixty seconds, and he immediately will ask for sexual intimacy. However, that just does not work for a majority of wives, because an emotional connection is an absolute must for most women before any sexual tenderness.

Most wives are not microwaves, nor are most husbands Crock-Pots. When a husband makes a spur-of-the-moment request with "Let's make love," his wife is thinking, "There is no way." At a minimum, most wives need to turn on their Crock-Pot in the morning or, even better yet, the night before the intimate con-nection. Thus, I encourage husbands to directly ask for sexual intimacy at least *twelve to hopefully twenty-four hours in advance*. This allows a wife to turn on the Crock-Pot so she is prepared and ready by the next night.

It is extremely important to be direct when using the *advance notice* or asking for sexual intimacy. Far too often, marriages are hurting in the sexual closeness area because there is only hinting given when intercourse is desired. Spouses become frustrated because their partner did not catch the "clue" that sexual inti-macy was being requested. Clues like lighting a candle, that spe-cial hug, the wink, a unique sensual touch may work most of the time, but far too often those "signals" are missed and the result is frustration.

In addition, always be considerate with your sexual intima-cy requests. I have counseled husbands who demanded sexual intimacy in the middle of the night, which is actually highly inconsiderate and perhaps emotional abuse. The *twelve to twenty-four hours advance notice* will negate spur-of-the-moment requests. The *advance notice* is indispensable because in nearly every marriage, one spouse desires sexual intimacy more than the other partner.

Finally, a major complaint from many husbands is, "I am tired of always asking for sexual intimacy." Some husbands will tell me that they want sexual activity to be spontaneous, but after the age of forty, that rarely happens, especially if you have children in your home. Husbands, please keep in mind that in happy marriages, 85 percent of the time the husband initiates sexual intimacy. If you are a husband, I understand that sentence may be disappointing to read, but nonetheless, most of the time in gratifying marriages the husband is the initiator. That being said, I encourage you wives to request sexual intimacy to help your husband feel loved.

ALWAYS REMEMBER that the *ten-minute eye-to-eye heart talk, meaningful hug* and *lingering kiss, twelve quick connects*, and *four daily essentials* make a significant difference in the area of sexual intimacy. Your sexual intimacy can be incredibly enjoyable, and it is a major component to marital happiness! So be open to improving and growing in your sexual expression with each other throughout your married life.

34. SCHEDULE CLOSENESS AND ANSWER KEY QUESTIONS

The more you experience nude affection, the more both of you will desire that pleasure and sexual enjoyment on a regular basis. Regular nude, sensual touch, as well as regular sexual intercourse, bonds and connects you more tightly together. Unfortunately, the reverse is also true, where a lack of nude closeness often creates an emotional distance. So when it comes to nude closeness or any form of sexual intimacy—just do it.

With any type of self-improvement—losing weight, exercise, a better sleep schedule—you will initially feel uncomfortable. Likewise, if you do not feel uncomfortable, you are not changing, improving, and growing in the area of sexual intimacy or any of these *Simple Habits*. To help overcome those uncomfortable feelings, ask yourself three questions:

1. What is the best that can happen?
2. What is the worst that can happen?
3. Can I live with the worst?

I hope you will agree with this statement: "I can live with risking improvement so that I look forward to enriching all areas of our sexual affection." **Begin today!**

A majority of happy couples *schedule* sensual or sexual activity. Yes, that is correct—schedule nude bonding time together as well as intercourse! *Scheduling* allows you to focus on what is most important: touching, massaging, cuddling, stroking, hugging, and kissing. Perhaps schedule a ten-minute foot or back massage with no sexual touch to ignite your emotional connection. Some spouses misinterpret the biblical comment, "The wife does not have [exclusive] authority over her own body, but the husband shares with her; and likewise the husband does not have [exclusive] authority over his body, but the wife shares with him." (1 Corinthians 7:4 AMP) The 1 Corinthians passage is often misinterpreted and leads to demanding sexual intimacy whenever wanted. *Scheduling* may counter inconsiderate ultimatums for sexual intimacy that are often the result of misunderstanding this passage from 1 Corinthians.

At a minimum, nude closeness on a weekly basis is the ultimate goal. Even if you do not have sexual intercourse, relaxing in the nude together will help you develop a stronger emotional bond. You could also take a shower or bath together on a regular basis.

Furthermore, take your time with physical affection. Set aside fifteen to thirty minutes when scheduling your nude closeness. Perhaps just lie in the nude in bed while watching a television show together. One wife told me, "That will never work because my husband will have to have intercourse." If you both agree to only nude closeness, then you need to fulfill your promise of just that—without sexual activity.

At times, intercourse is not an option for a marriage. Some spouses may have excruciating back pain, some type of significant physical discomfort, or a health issue that will not allow for intercourse. In addition, some husbands may be impotent while some wives might have physical ailments, and thus intercourse is not an option. For whatever reason, if intercourse is not an option, I still encourage you to have meaningful nude physical touch just for the love, appreciation, warmth, value, and relationship enhancement it provides. Lying with each other in the nude will also help you relax, destress, and improve your physical well-being.

Finally, always be open-minded and willing to experiment with various forms of godly physical touch. In that regard, answer the following essential questions and then discuss your answers together:

1. During the last year, describe your most romantic sexual intimacy interlude and what made it special for you.
2. In the area of making love, the two verbal phrases you most like to hear are . . . .
3. In the area of making love, the two verbal phrases you really dislike to hear are . . . .
4. In the area of making love, two behaviors or actions you wish your partner would demonstrate more often are . . . .
5. In the area of making love, two behaviors or actions you wish your partner would avoid are . . . .

6. From the initial request for sexual intimacy through the end of your closeness together, describe your "perfect" romantic experience.

7. What obstacles do you as a couple need to overcome to increase your satisfaction with your sex life?

Lastly, be adventurous by giving new sexual experiences at least two attempts to evaluate the pleasure and perhaps the potential for growth in your relationship.

I want to repeat that you may need to feel uncomfortable with new intimacy behaviors to gain that comfortable, safe feeling, but the payoff is significant for your marriage. Improve your sexual intimacy by striving for only 1 percent improvement per week or even per month, and delight in meeting your spouse's sexual intimacy needs.

CHAPTER IV

COMMUNICATION HABITS THAT BUILD UP A MARRIAGE

Almighty God has wonderful wisdom regarding *communication*: "Do not let unwholesome talk come out of your mouths, but only what is helpful for building others up according to their needs, that it may benefit those who listen" (Ephesians 4:29 NIV), and "The tongue of the wise speaks knowledge that is pleasing and acceptable, but the [babbling] mouth of fools spouts folly" (Proverbs 15:2 AMP).

In the first counseling session for a troubled marriage, I always ask both spouses what they view as the main problem in the relationship. Almost 100 percent of the time, one or both will say it is communication. A decline of emotional oneness and a lack of good communication go together. It is well known that *communication problems* are often cited as the most common factor that leads to divorce.

Keep in mind, too, that we cannot *not* communicate. Even silence by a spouse is a form of communication that leads to folly. Silence indicates either anger in the heart or that the other partner is just not important enough for words.

The word *communicate* comes from the Latin word *communicare*, meaning "to share" or "to make common." Regular sharing of nurturing words coupled with positive actions is essential for marital happiness, and this chapter gives you the necessary skills for repairing or preventing broken communication and elevating your marital satisfaction. *Communication* goes hand in hand with enhancing close companionship as well as with developing emotional intimacy.

35. THE BIG "E": EXPECTATIONS

More than likely you and your spouse married because *your expectations* were being met on a regular, if not daily basis. While dating, having your expectations satisfied was extremely rewarding, and you probably felt so wonderful being continually gratified, you wanted that feeling the rest your life.

Whenever you are satisfied in your marriage, the simple reason is that your expectations are being met. Whenever you are disappointed in your marriage, the reverse is true, and your expectations are not being fulfilled. Furthermore, most marital heartaches stem from *unexpressed expectations*. Very simply, *expectations* will either create a strong emotional connection or deep disappointment and hurt. Your marital satisfaction or dissatisfaction is all about the BIG "E": EXPECTATIONS! Hence, within the first two sessions for every premarital couple and troubled marriage, I explain the importance of *expectations*.

Nearly thirty years ago, I counseled a struggling couple that had been married for thirty-two years. Both spouses wanted a divorce, and the sooner the better for each of them. This faithful Christian couple attended weekly worship services, so their pastor was shocked when the couple made an appointment to tell him about their impending divorce. The pastor gave them my name and asked that they not divorce until they had spent several sessions with me.

The very first session I thoroughly explained *expectations*: helping them identify what they expected of one another and how that would lead to satisfaction, explaining how their expectations needed to be realistic and reasonable, teaching them how to *request expectations,* encouraging them to make their expectations specific, and then urging both of them to do everything possible to meet their spouse's expectations. At the end of that first session, I also asked them to request an *expectation* from each other on a daily basis for a week.

When the couple returned for their second session, both had smiles on their faces and reported being much happier. Both partners reported that all fourteen expectation requests had been positively fulfilled and that created a gratifying week. The wife said, "We are putting our divorce on hold, and we want to continue learning the *Simple Habits* for lifelong happiness." Thankfully I can share that this couple not only learned and regularly implemented *Simple Habits*, but several years ago also celebrated their sixtieth wedding anniversary.

When you have most of your *expectations* met by your spouse, you have a strong emotional bond and you feel valued. When your expectations are not fulfilled, you usually have painful heartache and heartburn. So it is absolutely essential that both of you specifically clarify in your own mind what words and behaviors create a healthy, rewarding marriage relationship. It will be very difficult to have a gratifying relationship without your expectations being satisfied.

Some examples for unmet expectations include the following:

1. A hurting wife shared with her husband how deeply disappointed she was over his visits to strip clubs. His response: "Strip clubs are not illegal, so I will continue to frequent those adult establishments."

2. A wife told her husband, "I want peace and quiet every holiday, with no visits from family and friends." The husband felt heartache and great disappointment because his expectation for holidays included social occasions with family and friends.

3. A husband told his wife he would like the two of them to take a one-week vacation every four months. The wife

replied, "I am happy just doing projects around our house and spending each evening in our four-season room. I do not want to leave our city."

These husbands and wives had ongoing disappointment with unfulfilled expectations, and the three couples continued with troubled, unhappy relationships.

Your number-one job is to identify and then communicate your *expectations* in each area of your relationship. Keep your expectations *reasonable and specific*. I understand that each of you has your own personal dictionary of defined words. What is reasonable for one of you may not be reasonable for the other spouse. However, don't have an expectation that no spouse could ever fulfill. Thus, my definition of *reasonable* includes words and behaviors that would be demonstrated by a healthy spouse within a gratifying marriage.

A major roadblock to healthy communication is expecting your spouse to know your wants and needs without you making a request. I have yet to meet a spouse who can read minds. So never make your spouse guess what you expect of them. Most fights and arguments are caused by unexpressed expectations. Your spouse cannot anticipate your wants and needs.

When you do not tell your partner your *expectations*, you often start to blame them for your unhappiness. This ineffective communication interferes with your closeness. Unknown expectations not only create tension but add to the stress if you begin accusing them for their lack of understanding and love for you. However, your unhappiness is actually your mistake because you did not ask your spouse for what you expect from them.

Insignificant issues often contribute to most marital heartaches, and the truly sad thing is that these small rubs could be overcome if *expectations* about daily trivialities were made known. Your relationship will also significantly struggle when you repeatedly make your expectations known, but your spouse for whatever reason ignores them. Thus, if either one of you thinks, "I meet my spouse's expectations, but my spouse has no interest whatsoever in meeting my expectations," you are living in the danger zone of divorce.

Some spouses have told me that they really don't have any expectations. However, every spouse has hundreds of *expectations*, but for some partners it can be very difficult to recognize exactly what you expect will lead to a satisfying marriage. For example, I often ask, "Do you expect your spouse to be faithful?" "Do you expect your spouse to rob a bank?" "Do you expect your spouse to have $100,000 in credit card debt?" Certainly, the answers to those questions are quite obvious, but the questions reinforce my point that you have numerous expectations.

I suggest you write down your *top ten expectations* in the major aspects of your relationship. Your expectations need to be reasonable, with godly words and behaviors. Perhaps you may even want to prioritize your top ten. With your list of *top ten expectations*, create S.M.A.R.T expectations that are: Specific, Measurable, Attainable, Realistic, and Time-oriented.

Some expectation questions to consider include: How do I want us to make decisions with major purchases? How important is budgeting for me? How often do I want to go out to eat? How often will we take a mini-vacation or vacation? How often will we turn off the television and just talk with each other? How important are birthday and anniversary cards? You might also consider the following among your list of *top ten expectations:* faith and worship, decision-making, extended family relationships, recreation, sexual intimacy, physical touch, friendships, household roles, birthdays, holidays, self-time, sleep schedules, gifts, etc.

In order to give properly to each other, you must know what your spouse expects of you. Thus, after completing your lists, share your *top ten expectations* with each other. By fully understanding what your spouse expects of you, you now have targets at which to aim. This exercise will also help you evaluate just how happy the two of you will potentially be in your marriage. The more expectations both of you can meet from your top ten list, the more gratification you will receive from your relationship.

The best way to strengthen your marital bond happens through meeting *expectations*. Engage your spouse with daily requests for what you expect in order to provide opportunities for loving each other. When your *expectations* are met, you will feel valued and special. And meeting your spouse's expectations is not only a privilege, but a sign of your love and commitment.

36. MAKE REQUESTS, NOT DEMANDS

Jesus urges us to "ask" in Matthew 7:7: "Ask and keep on asking and it will be given to you" (AMP), and the apostle Paul encourages us to make our specific requests known to God in Philippians 4:6 (AMP): "Do not be anxious or worried about anything, but in everything [every circumstance and situation] by prayer and petition with thanksgiving, continue to make your [specific] requests known to God." Every happy couple I have ever counseled was above average in regular *asking* with *specific requests* for their wants and needs.

It may seem like a little thing, but whenever you make an expectation known to your spouse, it is very important to put it in the form of a question rather than a sentence. Polite questions or requests allow your spouse the personal freedom to make a decision. Sentences, on the other hand, come across as demands, commands, or even orders. A *request* usually does not come across as a selfish demand, but a neutral need or want that will actually increase marital satisfaction.

Over the years of helping couples, I have noticed that troubled marriages often involve spouses who make demands regarding their expectations and needs. Usually it involves comments like: "Do this," "Do that," or "Give me this." Even when using the rule of courtesy with a statement: "Please take out the trash." Such a sentence can create a feeling of being ordered around without the chance to say "No."

We all want to be in charge of our life and have personal freedom to make our own choices. Statements not only remove the feeling of choice but can also easily be interpreted as an attack. No healthy individual likes forfeiting their personal independence. A *request*, on the other hand, allows for a "Yes" or "No" answer, and your spouse feels more in control of their individual autonomy.

I think the best way to make an expectation known is with the question, *"Will you please?"* I realize that you could also ask "Would you please?" but I believe psychologically the word "will" is softer on the ears and implies a more positive intent. I would also avoid "Could you please?" and "Can you please?" So, use "will" versus "would," "could," or "can."

In addition, be extremely aware of the importance placed upon your tone of voice and your body language when asking, *"Will you please?"* Your mannerisms, a soft tone of voice, and a warm facial expression will definitely influence how your spouse receives your request. One spouse told me, "When we use a 'Will you please' with each other, it automatically adds more politeness and a higher level of civility to our relationship."

If you still prefer to use a sentence with "Please do this," or "Please do that," always end with a question like, "Is that all right with you?" or "What do you think about that?" This is often called the "Say-Ask" communication skill. For example, "I would like to go on a date this Friday night at 6:00 p.m. Is that all right with you?" By ending with a question after your sentence, your spouse will not feel commanded, because he or she still has a choice. They can make a decision to say either "Yes" or "No" and maintain their personal freedom.

When you have an expectation, understand the importance of a window of time for a response. Generally, it is not healthy to require expectations to be completed immediately. For example, if you want something done around the house that may take thirty minutes, allow your spouse at least a half day or more to complete the request. If your *"Will you please"* takes ten minutes or less, give your spouse a few hours for meeting your expectation. If your *"Will you please"* takes an hour or more, give your partner at least a few days for completing the task. Always provide enough time so your spouse is not feeling ordered around. Finally, only make one or two *"Will you please"* requests each day. Making numerous *"Will you please"* requests on a daily basis can come across as a string of demands.

Expectations affect nearly every area of your marriage. It's important to make your expectations known. But remember to **make requests with your expectations**, not immediate demands.

37. WATCH YOUR TONE, BODY LANGUAGE, AND PRONOUNS

What impacts your communication the most is how you speak to your spouse. Your *tone of voice* and *body language* make an immense difference in determining your level of contentment in your marriage. I have heard thousands of times, "It is not what my spouse says, but *how they say it.*" Or, "My spouse comes across as brash, abrupt, discourteous, rude, impolite, etc." Or, "My spouse speaks at me in an angry, condescending tone of voice." When you speak to your spouse, approximately 40 percent of your message comes through your *tone of voice* and over 50 percent is your *body language*. Thus, both a warm tone of voice and a kind facial expression make a huge difference in daily marital satisfaction. Regularly ask yourself, "Are my *tone and body language* healing or hurting my desire for marital oneness?"

I suggest you speak with your spouse just like you talk to a dog. When I gently pet a dog and at the same time slowly speak the warm, soft words, "You are a very brutal, mean, and vicious beast," the result would be an extremely relaxed, comforted dog because the dog did not hear the words, only my kind tone of voice, demeanor, and body language. On the other hand, I could move my hand up and down like I was going to hit the dog and at the same time say in a fast, loud, and cruel-sounding voice, "You are a very compassionate, caring, and lovable pet." The outcome would be entirely different, and the dog would cower in fear of being hit and abused.

Likewise, your spouse does not really hear the words from your message as much as he or she interprets your content from the inflection of your voice along with your body gestures or facial looks. Too often I have heard, "The look of disgust and disdain really turned me off. It is definitely not their words but their tone and facial expression." When expressing your thoughts and feelings with your spouse, I encourage you to use the attributes of Jesus—compassion and humility. As one spouse said, "A warm tone of voice coupled with a caring facial expression helps the message to be digested easier."

Finally, always watch your *pronoun language*! In God's eyes, you have a one-flesh union. So always use *we* or *our* or *us* and NOT *my*. After counseling thousands of spouses, I have discovered that troubled couples use the pronoun *my* frequently rather than *our* or *we* or *us*. One wife told me, "Until you pointed out that pronoun language was so very important, I never realized how incredibly disappointing and hurtful it was to hear my husband rarely say *our* but almost always say *my*."

Pronoun language seems like a small thing, but the *we* and *our* creates the feeling of being united together for a lifetime. Thus, it is not my home but *our* home; not my car but *our* car; and not my money but *our* money. *Will you please* allow your pronouns to unite and strengthen your marriage?

38. SPEAK THE TRUTH IN LOVE

Many couples have miserable relationships because one or both spouses speak the truth, but it is often a vicious and brutal truth rather than given in love. Ephesians 4:15 declares, "But speaking the truth in love [in all things—both our speech and our lives expressing His truth]" (AMP). So yes, God wants spouses to speak the truth, but they should *always do it in love*.

When we talk with our partner, doing so *in love* happens through what's known as an "I Message." You may have learned about the importance for using phrases that start with "I," rather than "You," when expressing your hurts and disappointments. "I Messages" are a gentler, softer way to express your feelings, thoughts, and opinions without attacking your spouse.

Hiding your negative feelings from your spouse may only increase the emotional distance between the two of you. So, when something is bothering you, *speak the truth in love*. A husband once told me that during their twenty-five years of marriage, he and his wife were always pleasant and had never had even a minor disagreement. But sadly, their relationship was superficial and not emotionally close. One of the reasons that satisfying marriages are so happy is because both spouses *do* share hurts and disappointments rather than bottle up those negative feelings. And the sharing of negative feelings will actually help manifest more positive words and actions in your relationship.

If you are unable to share with each other your hurts and disappointments, your marriage will have significant struggles. In unhappy relationships, I hear comments like, "I don't think my spouse will ever be able to handle a *speak the truth in love* expression"; "My spouse gets really upset when I share even a minor disappointment"; and "If I ever share a hurt, my spouse will make sure I pay for it by withholding sex, or being passive-aggressive by refusing to do a necessary task, or just plain being extra-vicious and brutal with words."

Pent-up negative emotions can eventually build a resentment force so intense the marriage comes apart at the seams. Figuratively, it's as if all spouses have a gunnysack over their shoulder. When a hurt or disappointment is experienced, it is thrown in the gunnysack. If the gunnysack fills up and eventually weighs like a bag of concrete, you become pressed down and want to leave the sack behind, meaning to perhaps end the relationship. In a healthy way, regularly keep your gunnysack empty by *speaking the truth in love* to release those painful emotions.

This simple four-step formula benefits you through pausing so you think before you speak. Hence, you are able to share your disappointments and hurts in a nicer way. This method not only expresses the "I Message" in a more caring manner, but it also offers a solution.

The first step identifies what is bothering you, either words or actions. Begin by stating, "When I heard . . ." if the hurt is a word, or "When I saw . . ." if the disappointment is a behavior.

For the second step, express your feelings by using either the words *hurt* or *disappointed*. If a deep heartache occurred, then use both *hurt and disappointed*. When the issue is especially painful, you may want to add the word "really" before "hurt and disappointed." But never use blocking words like *frustrated, upset, angry, bitter, mad, resentful*, or any other strong negative words that could build a significant wall between the two of you. It is extremely important to use just *hurt, disappointed*, or *hurt and disappointed*.

Third, give *specific reasons* for your hurt or disappointment. A lighthearted example would be:

1. *"When I saw* you leave the toilet seat up"
2. *"I felt disappointed"*
3. *"Because* I was scared I would fall in the toilet if I used the bathroom in the middle of the night."

Finally, if you only use the first three steps without offering a solution, you are basically only interested in complaining. Per the business world motto, "Don't bring me a problem unless you have a solution," offer a possible solution in the form of a request with a "*Will you please..?*"

Another example:

1. "*When I rarely see* you cook during the week"
2. "*I feel hurt and disappointed*"
3. "*Because* I work full-time and you work part-time two days per week."
4. "*Will you please* cook dinner on the three days you don't work and we can each take a day cooking on the weekends?"

When the response is a positive "Yes," your hurt is resolved, and your marital satisfaction will be enhanced. If your spouse's answer is "No," both of you can discuss your reasons and perspective in more detail. As you seek to understand each other's viewpoint, hopefully a compromise can be found that will satisfy both of you. One spouse told me, "When I became more assertive with the four-step *speak the truth in love* formula, my spouse became more considerate and started meeting my expectations." So before speaking the truth in love, sometimes it is beneficial to practice out loud what you want to say.

Again, do not bottle up your hurts and disappointments, but regularly share your inner feelings and thoughts using *speak the truth in love.*

39. TWO CONSECUTIVE QUESTIONS

Jesus asked more than three hundred questions in the Bible. Jesus knew the importance of asking questions in order to look deep inside a person. Jesus' questions often drew Him closer to those around Him, as well as providing insights into the fact that He was the Messiah, the Savior.

How often has your spouse, a family member, or a friend asked you a question just because they wanted to launch into a discussion of what was on their mind? For example, individuals frequently ask, "How was your day?" Even if you respond with "Horrible," that person then goes on to describe in detail what *their* day was like, with little concern for the reasons your own day was "horrible."

One way to become a great listener is to ask *two consecutive questions.* Such a guideline forces you to have an interest in your spouse's life, thus strengthening your marriage. Whenever you are apart and reconnect, have the guideline that both of you will ask each other *two questions* about your day. First, you might ask the simple question, "How was your day?" A second question might possibly be, "What can I do to make your evening more enjoyable?" If the request is reasonable, meet your spouse's request and create a pleasant evening together.

Think of your first question as just a warm-up question for the all-important second question. The second question is the significant one and really bonds you to your partner. The second question also shows your spouse just how much you value them and how important their thoughts, feelings, and life are to you.

Hopefully, you can implement the *two consecutive questions* guideline while sitting down. Remember, your eyes are the windows to your spouse's heart. When you have a *heart connection*, it is much easier to deal with daily stress. By remembering to *double your interest* through a second question, you value your spouse and demonstrate a commitment to help your spouse feel important. So, whether standing or sitting, look into your spouse's eyes and *ask two questions* to show an interest in your spouse's life, thereby strengthening your emotional bond.

40. MARRIAGE CONNECTORS

A positive connection is essential for both a good marriage and your physical and emotional well-being. At times, you may not have any idea what is truly important to your spouse. In counseling, spouses will often say, "I had no clue that 'such and such' really mattered to you." Thus, when you are drifting apart, I offer several simple sentence completion suggestions to help reconnect you.

First, I encourage you to utilize these key phrases on a regular basis when you are seeking improvement in your marriage. The two similar phrases are: "*I really need. . .*" and "*It is really important to me . . .* " Being specific and exact with those two phrases will help your spouse understand what you need in order for you to be emotionally bonded together. A second idea for strengthening your relationship and reinforcing what is truly meaningful for you about your spouse's words and behaviors is to tell your spouse "*I really love . . . about you.*" Reaffirming what you sincerely like about your spouse, whether words or behaviors, will encourage your partner to manifest those actions even more in the future.

Whenever you and your spouse are drifting apart emotionally, use these *marriage connectors* to restore your emotional connection. There is no better way to reconnect than a heart-to-heart conversation sharing your specific needs via the *marriage connectors* as well as telling your spouse what you really appreciate about them.

Again, your main marital goals are to overcome complacency, defeat bad habits, and achieve greater emotional oneness. Hence, both of you are responsible for making requests that will benefit your marriage. So regularly use these *marriage connectors* to avoid taking each other for granted and strengthen your relationship.

CHAPTER V

HABITS THAT GUARD YOUR RELATIONSHIP

J esus warns, "Keep actively watching and praying that you may not come into temptation; the spirit is willing, but the body is weak" (Matthew 26:41 AMP). Generally speaking, it is a falsehood that both spouses contribute to a divorce, because that is true only a small percentage of the time. It takes two healthy spouses, *watching and guarding their behaviors* to make a satisfying relationship, and just one unhealthy spouse to break the happiness connection in a marriage.

Every spouse has both flaws and virtues, but what can break your emotional connection are one or more *intolerable flaws—* aka deal breakers. Intolerable flaws severely crack a marital foundation. An intolerable flaw or deal breaker is more than an annoying behavior; it is a detrimental habit that causes marital anguish. Many divorces occur because a spouse has at least one intolerable flaw. I am not suggesting that you have to be perfect, but both of you need to guard your relationship by continually seeking improvement and growth in all marital areas.

This chapter may be difficult, because as you look in the mirror, you might have to face a particular intolerable flaw that is producing ongoing unhappiness in your marriage. Without recognizing an intolerable flaw, however, creating a gratifying marriage will be a huge challenge. Hence, if either of you refuse to see the problems created by an intolerable flaw, you won't improve your individual behavior, much less your marital satisfaction. Hopefully, with the knowledge from this chapter, you will be able to recognize and defeat any deal breakers in order to have a rewarding relationship.

41. LEAVE AND CLEAVE

God's Word states that all healthy couples must demonstrate a *leave and cleave* (see Genesis 2:24) mentality by leaving their former family unit and establishing a new one-flesh union. Without a healthy *leaving*, rarely will there be a healthy *cleaving* for a satisfying marriage. When you don't cut the umbilical cord, trouble lies ahead. Thus, your goal is to relate to all family members from a healthy physical and emotional distance. Jesus said, "Love your neighbor as yourself" (Mark 12:31 AMP), and your closest neighbor is now your spouse, NOT your parents. Once you marry, you no longer need a "mommy" and a "daddy" but now a mother and a father.

One of the main reasons you decided to have lifelong companionship was your desire to spend time together. The two of you made a commitment to God to have Christ as your first loyalty, and second, each other. Your primary focus is on daily togetherness with your spouse, NOT with your mother or father. If either of you are overly attached to a parent, that can be a danger signal for significant marriage problems in more than one area of your relationship. A physical, emotional, and yes technological separation from your parents is not just necessary *but essential* for a satisfying, enjoyable marriage. Thus, in terms of importance, I place this lesson in the top three habits, because *you must separate* from your parents in order to have lifelong happiness with your spouse.

Healthy parents teach their children to be independent and self-reliant, helping those children learn to do things for themselves. Parents are always parents, but healthy parents also realize the importance of encouraging their grown-up children to make a smooth transition to independent adulthood. Wholesome parents recognize that the main goal of parenting is to work themselves out of a job. Hopefully your parents recognize they have now "'retired" from parenting. This comment is often especially difficult for mothers who see parenting as their only identity and purpose in life.

Let me explain further—your parents should not make their life about you. Some parents have a goal for continual dependency by having daily conversations either on the phone, on social media, in text messages, or even in person.

With many troubled marriages, I have frequently heard, "My wife is very dependent on her mother and more emotionally connected to her mom than me. Now that we are married, my wife should have a mother, instead she still has a 'mommy.' Several times each day, my wife and her mother speak, text, or connect through social media, and sadly, my wife spends more time with 'mommy' than me"; "My husband continually contacts his dad looking for approval and acknowledgment, and it feels like he is married to his dad not me"; "Our teenage daughters said to my wife, 'You talk to your mom an unusual amount of time. Please realize we are not going to call you two or three times every day when we are married'"; and "My husband texts his mom several times during the day, she often calls him, and treats him like a little boy." Of course, I have heard similar comments made by both husbands and wives.

Your parents need to focus on their marriage, personal life, or perhaps other children still under their care, but not you and your marriage! If you have an overly involved parent, you probably are thinking two questions that I have been asked numerous times. One, "Why would my mother/father either unintentionally or intentionally hurt my marriage?" And second, "What are the reasons that my parent does not focus more on their own personal life or marriage?"

Parents who are overly involved in the lives of their married children often do so for two reasons. First, their personal lives are not satisfying and therefore they seek life fulfillment through enmeshed, almost smothering interaction with their adult children. Or second, the parent's marriage is broken and not satisfying. Thus, they try to achieve relationship satisfaction by being overly attached to their adult children and their families. Parents who continue to live for an extremely close connection with their adult children are not healthy and can tremendously damage a marriage.

If either one of you has not *left* your parents, or if your parents want to be extremely entangled in your life and marriage, pray for the wisdom of Solomon as you seek solutions for a healthy physical and emotional distance. Key questions to ask yourself include: "Do I *have to* talk with either of my parents almost daily?" "On a daily and weekly basis, how much contact time do I have with my parents?" And, "Am I satisfied with physical contact and talks just every so often with my parents?" Answer these questions together and work for goals that will satisfy both of you.

Without a *healthy separation*, physically and emotionally, from your parents, it is almost impossible to have a happy, satisfying marriage. In fact, one of the significant factors for determining marital success will be the degree to which you have emotionally and physically separated from your parents.

Always remember, your closest connection is now your spouse. So *leaving your parents* is absolutely essential for a gratifying marriage. Without a healthy balance in *leaving your parents and cleaving to one another*, a pleasing marriage will be a significant challenge. *Thus, strongly desire to seek primary love, comfort, and bonding from each other—**not your parents!***

42. RECOGNIZE YOUR FALSE BELIEFS

Bringing two backgrounds together for a satisfying marriage is a challenge for every couple because both of you have different opinions on what are the "truths of life." Healthy thinking leads to healthy behaviors! However, unhealthy thinking often reinforces *false truths*, which can create significant marital heartaches.

Sadly, the Pharisees held to false beliefs and did not even recognize Jesus as the Son of God, the Messiah promised in the Old Testament, and the Savior of the world. In Matthew 23, Jesus pronounced woes upon their false religion, false teachings, and false beliefs. Likewise, a marriage will often have "troubling woes" if one or both spouses has one or more *false beliefs*.

I define a *false belief* or *incorrect truth* as a flawed understanding or untrue perception in any facet of the marriage. Please be aware that a *false belief* is actually an *unintentional impairment* or *block* in accurately understanding an aspect of a marital relationship that would create marital happiness. No matter the reason, a spouse with a flawed belief will be unable to function in a healthy manner in that particular facet of the marriage.

Like most spouses, both of you regularly exhibit both healthy and unhealthy behaviors, then those behaviors form habits, and those habits shape your marriage. The negative habits, even small ones, are often at the core of your marital dissatisfaction. Please answer honestly two difficult questions: "Could some of my perceptions about life be wrong?" and "Can I identify my *false truths* or *false beliefs* that may actually hurt our marital satisfaction?"

Your core beliefs often form a marital picture for what you think your marriage should look like. In childhood, you learned core beliefs from your parents, stepparents, grandparents, and significant others. From those individuals closest to you, you developed marital ideas about finances, faith, household roles, affection, faithfulness, praise, attitude, hugs, kisses, etc. Unfortunately, the core beliefs you learned from others may be

false truths. If you build your life and marriage around core beliefs that are *false truths*, the result will be marital disappointment and heartache.

Too many spouses rely on their instincts rather than proven
facts, thereby destroying their marriage. Perhaps as you read
Simple Habits for Marital Happiness, you may question a number
of the suggested habits; they may just not make sense based upon
what you learned from childhood. You may not agree with every
idea in this book, but please understand these behaviors have
helped over a thousand couples have satisfying relationships.
Since over 50 percent of marriages fail and probably more than
three-fourths of married individuals are dissatisfied and unhappy, it will be extremely important to assess your core beliefs and
then identify those viewpoints that are actually *false truths* that
harm your marital relationship.

Whenever a spouse tells me that they don't agree with some
of the habits from *Simple Habits for Marital Happiness*, their marriage usually is unhappy. One husband said, "I am like my dad. He
was a jerk, but my mom and dad never divorced so why should
I change?" His wife responded, "Your mom is only a shell of a
woman, a doormat, and we are headed toward divorce." A wife
said, "My mom was controlling and dominant and my parents are
not divorced, so why should I improve upon my bad habits?" A
husband shared, "My parents were opinionated and confronted
issues with just brutal honesty." Sadly, his wife said, "Your parents are often vicious and cruel with their comments and neither
one likes the other." I could share hundreds of quotes from mis-
guided spouses. My goal is to help you understand that your *false
beliefs* may cause you to think that some of the healthy behaviors
from this book are rubbish. If those are your thoughts, I believe
your marriage may struggle with numerous disappointments.

The first step is to identify what you think are beneficial beliefs about marriage that you learned from significant others in
childhood. Make a list of those top ten virtues and behaviors from

noteworthy individuals who mentored you growing up. Your list should include attributes that led to a successful individual life or a gratifying marital relationship of thirty-five years or more. Next, discuss with your spouse why you think those attributes, qualities, or actions are worth incorporating into your life and marriage. You may discover that your spouse thinks some of those beliefs are really *false truths*.

The next step will be more difficult because we frequently do not want to see toxic negatives in those we value. I am always amazed at how challenging it is to take off the blinders, overcome our prejudices, and see shortcomings in those we love. One way to assist in this process is to remember as a teenager or young adult what annoyed you the most about your mother and father's marriage. It might help for both of you to actually write down your parents' marital issues that you really want to overcome.

Without recognizing those "defects" in significant others that you want to avoid, a satisfying marriage will be difficult. The reason is that you will be incorporating *false beliefs* in your relationship. Just acknowledging your parents' or stepparents' shortcomings will place you on the road to a better relationship because you will be headed in a positive direction. Please, for the sake of your marriage, widely open your eyes and identify those incorrect beliefs that must be avoided at all cost.

Truthful beliefs will set you free, improving your life and making your marital relationship happier. However, incorporating *truthful beliefs* in your relationship may cause you to feel uncomfortable and perhaps even confused as you implement those healthier life and relationship principles. In the next lesson, I will describe individual issues and agonizing shortcomings that are destructive personally as well as for your marriage.

43. DEAL WITH SIGNIFICANT PERSONAL ISSUES

According to Christian tradition, there are seven deadly sins: envy, gluttony, greed, lust, pride, laziness, and anger. These seven deadly sins are troubling issues, but there are other personal problems that can lead to marital heartache, as well. Whether it is a troubling individual issue or a more serious personality disorder, individual problems are challenging for your marriage.

In addition, if you are not personally happy, it is very unlikely that you will be happily married. Your individual happiness is up to you, not your spouse. Always remember: Two healthy, contented individuals make a satisfying marriage, but it only takes one unhealthy spouse to break the marital oneness or make it extremely miserable.

If you or your spouse has a *significant personal issue*, it is very important to seek professional Christian counseling, read an excellent self-help book, or both. My goal in this lesson is not to resolve any individual issues or personality disorders you may have, but only to help you understand that some distressed relationships are not really caused by marital issues but by personal problems.

A happy individual can be a happy spouse, but an unhappy individual will almost never be a happy spouse. In that regard, one spouse sadly stated, "I do whatever it takes to keep my partner happy, but I now realize that they will never be happy either with themselves or our marriage." If you or your partner agrees with some form of this statement, "my spouse is an unbalanced person due to emotional baggage from past experiences," then one of you may have personal struggles where improvement is absolutely necessary. In the next paragraphs, I provide examples of significant personal issues.

I counseled a couple where the wife refused to physically touch her husband in any way—no peck kisses, no quick hugs, no hand-holding, absolutely no touching of any kind! Intercourse had not occurred in four years. Coincidentally, he also did 90 percent of all of the household chores. The husband was one of the finest Christian men I have ever met, so although he was not perfect, he was not the problem. Unfortunately, his wife's lack of physical touch and laziness with household chores were significant issues. Yet, his wife insisted they had marriage problems, not a personal issue.

With another couple I counseled, the husband called his wife horrible names, screamed at her constantly, and even hit her on occasion. Certainly, he demonstrated verbal, emotional, and physical abuse toward his wife. However, the husband did not take responsibility for his abuse, and he even said, "Our marriage has problems because my wife makes me behave that way." Another wife had a bizarre habit of always brushing her teeth within ten minutes after a meal. Hence, she never wanted to go to a restaurant with her husband for a *date your mate*. This was just one of many personal issues for this wife, yet she blamed their unhappy marriage on her husband.

One wife said, "My husband is intent on making everything horrible between us. When he comes through the door, he is absolutely woeful and seeks to make me miserable, as well. Trying to share my wants and needs with my husband is not only awkward, but a losing game." When she used the *speak the truth in love* formula to share her hurts, he became very angry and defensive. Another wife said, "My husband only wants to point fingers and complain that no one cares about how he feels. However, he almost never validates how I might be feeling."

Perhaps you walk on eggshells due to your spouse having a borderline personality disorder. Or perhaps your spouse has a histrionic personality disorder, needing to be the center of attention or a drama queen/king. Another major personality disorder is narcissism, in which a person is extremely self-absorbed. Your spouse may have anger or even rage issues. Or your spouse could be just extremely controlling by desiring to make a high percentage of all decisions. Or your spouse may have significant mood swings—extremely loving one day and for no apparent reason cold as ice the next day. Or your spouse may blame you and never accept responsibility for any shortcomings. Or your spouse may have anxiety issues and try to control everything in the marriage to diminish those nervous feelings. Some spouses with significant personal issues are constantly looking for attention or approval for completing even trivial tasks in the marriage.

Personally, you need to find happiness in your internal character qualities and what you do in life. You cannot rely on your spouse or your marriage for your contentment in life. Making an apple pie requires certain ingredients for a great-tasting pie. If you and your spouse are making the pie together, one of you may add sweet-tasting apples, and the other spouse may add the sugar as well as the other ingredients. However, if either of you were to add vinegar to the apple pie, the result would be a pie that tasted absolutely horrible.

Likewise, enhancing a marriage is a lot like making a delicious apple pie. Both of you need to be healthy individuals; in other words, you must possess pleasant-tasting "personal ingredients." If either of you have "personal ingredients" that taste like vinegar, you do not have marriage problems, but significant individual issues. Dealing with poisonous personal problems is a must!

The starting point is for you or your spouse to admit when you possess a "vinegar" issue and then have a strong desire to become healthier. Often, the main problem with a significant individual difficulty is that the "vinegar spouse" becomes defensive and refuses to recognize their problem and seek help. Or the unreasonable spouse will play the victim, saying, "I know I am the bad partner." With that statement, a spouse playing the victim role shamefully implies, "Pity me so I don't have to change."

If either of you has a major intolerable flaw, just the acknowledgment of that intolerable flaw is an important beginning. Nonetheless, *Simple Habits for Marital Happiness* is not a treatment plan for personality disorders or significant personal issues. Although there are no quick fixes or easy solutions, utilizing the behaviors from *Simple Habits for Marital Happiness* will help both of you become individually healthier spouses.

44. BE COOPERATIVE, NEVER CONTROLLING

Marriages are at their best when both spouses exhibit sympathy, empathy, humility, and compassion, all qualities possessed by Jesus. A spouse with those positive attributes at the core of their identity will regularly demonstrate kindness, patience, and cooperation within the relationship. Galatians 5:22–23 states, "But the fruit of the Spirit is love, joy, peace, patience, kindness, goodness, faithfulness, gentleness, self-control" (ESV). A spouse with self-control will usually possess a cooperative, collaborative spirit. Self-control, not other-control, is always the goal for a satisfying marriage.

The opposite of self-control is the negative *other-control*, which means *decision-control* and *relationship-control*. Definitely one of the most significant personal issues that can damage marital happiness is a *controlling spouse*. In public, a controlling spouse is usually engaging and pleasant, while in private they are passive-aggressive, temper-oriented, and highly stressful to be around. A *controlling spouse* is not only the opposite of easygoing, but is a very high-maintenance, challenging partner within a marital relationship. Sadly, the disease of control can be devastating to marital happiness.

A *controlling spouse* usually has anxiety and fears being out of control in almost any aspect of life, including the marriage. Often, the fear of losing control stems from a traumatic childhood event that created anxiety and an initial unmanageable feeling. The result for controllers is often low self-esteem, and thus persistent anxiety flows from that lack of self-worth. Most controlling spouses not only struggle with anxiety, but they may also wrestle with perfectionism, selfishness, depression, obsessive-compulsive personality disorder, or eating disorders. Sadly, *control fanatics* are continually not happy with themselves, their spouses, and yes, even their personal lives.

Regrettably, the more anxiety or insecure a spouse feels on the inside, the more other-control will be sought outside oneself. The myth for a control fanatic becomes, "If I can control every little thing, including my partner, my anxiety diminishes, and life will be perfect." One controlling spouse actually told me, "I must have control over all situations and all individuals, including my spouse, because I am so anxious and insecure that I will not allow myself to relax." A controlling spouse does not possess three important qualities for a satisfying life: *relaxation*, *fun*, and *enjoyment*.

Controlling actually *feels like it helps*, but it absolutely does not. In their minds, in order to make things go right in life, a controlling spouse seeks to organize and dominate their partner's life and the marital relationship. A controller lacks self-confidence and wrongfully thinks, "If I can control my spouse, other family members, and nearly every situation, that will be wonderful because my anxiety will greatly diminish." Even worse, more controlling behavior actually creates additional personal unhappiness, and of course, significant marital dissatisfaction.

Unfortunately, *controlling spouses* seldom have the ability to understand that they have an untrue perception of life and marriage. Due to living in a world of denial, a *control fanatic* will rarely admit to their controlling behavior, much less have the insight to recognize that a problem exists. *Control fanatics* have deficiencies in their thinking, believing they are more "righteous," which means to them, "I am always right, never wrong, and I know a lot more about life and relationships than everyone else." Since a controller falsely thinks they are always correct, they honestly believe their partner is somewhat of a "dummy" when it comes to life and marriage. So, most control fanatics believe that they alone have the real truths of life—but remember, they have an untrue perception of life! Therefore, *control fanatics* are the ones who are actually clueless within the marital relationship.

In order to feel relaxed, *control fanatics* seek to dominate their spouse, other family members, and significant aspects of the marriage, like major purchases, physical touch, recreational activities, vacations, and sexual intimacy—nearly everything that happens within the relationship. The outcome is that a *controlling spouse* usually creates a trembling partner, and that negatively affects marital satisfaction. The controlled partner often walks on eggshells because the controlling spouse again wrongly believes they alone have the "truth." A controlled partner usually has difficulty thinking independently and ends up losing personhood in life and the marriage. Sadly, a controlled spouse becomes almost a "yes" robot whose life purpose is only to serve their controlling partner.

Spouses who experience control by their partner will often make comments like: "When I don't say 'no' to my wife, she can be happy and nice. However, when my controlling wife hears any form of the word 'no,' she becomes unbearable, uncompromising, and very difficult"; "My husband is not willing to compromise, and I can't remember the last time he changed his mind"; "My wife is domineering, and once a week we have a discussion so I can be corrected and told what I am doing wrong"; "My husband will go to any lengths in order to NOT compromise"; "My wife is demanding and controls nearly every aspect of our marriage; simply put, she will do whatever she needs to do to achieve control"; "I don't do anything right, and my husband constantly corrects how I pay the bills, do the laundry, vacuum the floor, mow the grass, etc."; and finally, "My wife has an insatiable desire for control and being in charge of everything, hence she dismisses my opinions and decisions." If any of these statements describes you or your spouse, a *control fanatic* lives in your home.

Frequently, if either you or your spouse is a controlling partner, the marital outcome is "intimacy starvation" in several ways. Your marriage will be "starved" of sympathy, empathy, humility, and compassion. As one partner told me, "My husband is so controlling, conniving, and manipulative, he has almost no genuine kindness for me or others."

If a *control fanatic* is present, your relationship will also be starved of physical affection and regular sexual intimacy. Control fanatics usually manipulate frequency of sexual intimacy, and often that means intercourse only on an occasional basis. Due to anxiety, a controlling spouse may have a difficult time enjoying sexual freedom and will either blame their partner or make continual excuses for not wanting to enjoy sexual intimacy. Sexual enjoyment requires freedom from control. To fully participate in sexual intimacy requires both spouses to relax, let go of control, and enjoy God's gift of both physical and sexual touch—very difficult for a controller. One "intimacy-starved" husband told me, "When my wife withholds and 'starves' me, not only do I agonize personally, but I believe our marriage suffers."

If you struggle with being a *control fanatic*, understand that your internal anxiety, insecurities, and self-doubt are damaging your marital happiness. If you attempt to control almost every decision, please also realize that will only make things worse for you, your spouse, and your marriage. By learning to relax, have fun, compromise, be very easy to get along with, and stay open to a healthy balance with decision-making, you are not only helping yourself, but you are also significantly improving satisfaction within your relationship. On the other hand, if you live with a domineering spouse, your goal is to *manage your partner's control* by **nicely setting limits** with any controlling behaviors.

In conclusion, in a wholesome Christian marriage, both spouses **cooperate** with one another, meaning they are **easy to get along with and agreeable, NOT controlling**.

45. MUTUAL, FACT-BASED DECISION-MAKING

How well couples handle decisions is a vital determining factor in marital satisfaction. When it comes to making decisions, the goal for the outcome is to be both *mutual* and *fact-based*. In a happy marriage, two partners are reasonable and logical, working together in an objective manner to find solutions. The biblical principle for decisions is, "He who answers before he hears [the facts]—it is folly and shame to him" (Proverbs 18:13 AMP). When it comes to decisions, both partners need to evaluate the facts and eliminate feelings from the process.

The opposite of joint, shared choices is selfish, controlling self-interest. Per Lesson 44, many troubled marriages have one controlling spouse who usually makes most of the decisions within the home. Sadly, an anxious spouse does not advocate for objectivity or factual truth because nervous feelings dominate and often cause irrational "feeling" choices. Regrettably, controlling partners also have a tendency to be dramatic and go "over the top" when they are not allowed to make a particular decision. Dominating most of the marital choices bleeds over into ruling nearly every aspect of not only the marriage, but the other spouse's personal life choices, as well. An imbalance in major decision-making frequently leads to a broken, distressed relationship.

An effective marital *decision-making process* can actually enhance your relationship through the working-together process. Not all decisions are of equal importance, and many decisions are not "right" or "wrong." However, noteworthy decisions may truly impact your marital happiness or unhappiness for years, so keep your substantial choices in perspective for the sake of your relationship future. Examples of major decisions are: car or home purchases, vacations, entertainment, church home, where you live, landscaping, how money is spent, what type of décor is chosen for the home, mutual friends, and child-rearing practices.

Don't rush into making important decisions because it may take time to assemble all the facts.

A simple but effective way to assess the spousal percentage with decisions in all aspects of the marriage is for both of you to keep track of *every single decision made* in the marriage for one week. Please write down even the most minor choices that are made by either one of you. For example, include who controls the remote, who determines what you eat, who controls when the television is on and what television shows are watched, who decides when you eat out, who chooses what happens in the evenings, what you do on the weekend, etc. Literally, keep track of even the smallest choices that are made by each spouse. Such an exercise will speak volumes about your marital balance in decision-making.

To further illustrate, I once counseled a couple where the husband was absolutely controlled by his wife due to her making nearly every marital decision. She put rules on all aspects of their relationship, and when things did not go her way, she would overreact with anger, spiteful actions, or silence. Although he was only thirty-seven, the husband had significant health issues that I think were stress-related. His physical distress was likely tied to his wife's regulating his personal time as well as making most decisions within the relationship.

I shared that their marriage might benefit from an experiment in which each of them kept track of even the smallest decisions made for one week. Immediately, the husband said, "What a great idea!" But the wife quickly stated, "That is a stupid exercise, and I don't want to do it." When I asked her reasons, she replied, "After one week of recording every single decision, the results would indicate that I make at least 85 to 90 percent of our decisions, and I am absolutely not a control fanatic with our marital choices." This was a truly shocking comment that only validated her major denial. Unfortunately, the husband's health continued to be an ongoing problem under his wife's domination, and their relationship was equally unhappy.

With significant choices, always have a standard process where you mutually decide together upon the best option. Shown below is a very simple process for working together when making major decisions.

1. In one sentence, state the decision that needs to be addressed.
2. Each of you suggests one or two solutions.
3. Independently, make a written list of pros and cons for your solution(s).
4. Individually, write down three factual reasons for what you think is the best solution.
5. Discuss together your pros, cons, and three factual reasons—find areas of agreement.
6. Take your time—three days, three weeks, or three months—before taking any significant action.
7. Select a solution that you both can accept.

To have a relationship where both of you can feel satisfied, always share in the *decision-making process*, especially major decisions for both your personal and marital well-being. A mutual understanding with significant decisions frequently leads to a very gratifying marriage.

46. NO SECRETS OF ANY KIND

The Bible warns us, "For nothing is secret that will not be revealed, nor anything hidden that will not be known and come to light" (Luke 8:17 NKJV). There are no secrets from God, and there should be no secrets in a marriage, because almost all spousal secrets are eventually uncovered. to the detriment of the relationship. My definition of a "secret" is intentionally concealing the truth or withholding information from your spouse.

Very simply, *secrets* damage relationships, and healthy spouses do not have secrets. Secrets are both dishonest and are actually lies within a marriage. The moment a spouse begins keeping secrets, instantaneously deceit and betrayal are at the core of the relationship—and that is a dangerous warning sign for serious problems. Since the ultimate marital goal is oneness, why would a spouse ever have anything to hide?

Mates with integrity are truthful, trustworthy, and straightforward in all their activities. Spouses with high moral character have "no deceit" (Psalm 32:2 NIV), because deceit involves concealing important information from your spouse. Don't ever deceive your spouse because keeping a secret creates a division within your marriage.

With that said, you should never have anything to hide. When you are completely open with your spouse, then you will not have a problem with avoiding secrets. If an activity you are involved in needs to be a secret, it is not a healthy endeavor for your marriage. So, if either you or your spouse is not willing to share all passwords, provide access to cell phones, or share information about your whereabouts, it could be a sign that something harmful is occurring for your marriage relationship.

One wife said, "My husband does not need to know everything," but the truth is, she was having an affair. One husband shared, "It is none of my wife's business where I went for the evening and who I was with," but the reality is he was spending time with unhealthy friends at a gambling casino, leading to huge losses and significant marital debt. *Never* hiding what you are doing when you are away from your spouse will allow for the togetherness that unites you for lifelong happiness.

If you believe that your spouse is doing something unhealthy, it is not only understandable but permissible for you to check out what they are doing. The police are not allowed to come into your home without your permission. However, if the police believe that you are doing something criminal, then it is legal for them to seek a warrant and search your home. The same principle applies to your marriage.

First and foremost, each of you must never have any financial secrets; transparency with money is discussed more in the chapter on financial harmony. Second, you absolutely must not have technological secrets, involving e-mail, voice mail, cell phones, websites, etc. Today, I estimate that probably 25 percent of divorces occur as a result of social media. Each of you should have free access to each other's technology information in order for the foundation of trust to be strong.

To prevent temptation, many couples express their love and commitment for each other by sharing all passwords to their e-mail and other social media accounts. Sharing a password is also a powerful way to say that you want to trust each other and that you believe in your marriage. Perhaps creating identical passwords can be a way to build trust in your relationship.

When you do not have a similar password, then it is important for your spouse to have free access to check your e-mail or cell phone. A respectful way to allow for such an action is to say, "I am feeling a little uncomfortable, do you mind if I look at your cell phone, e-mail, etc.?"

Keeping *secrets* will only crack your marital foundation and dig a deep division between the two of you. Healthy couples just don't have *secrets*! Since a Christian strives to practice truthfulness in words and honesty in actions, secrets should never be an issue. Unite together by letting your spouse into your "entire world." And do whatever it takes to be completely open and *NEVER HAVE EVEN ONE SECRET!*

47. BE A GIVER; AVOID SELFISHNESS

The best gift you can give each other is the *gift of giving!* God's best gift was giving! "He *gave* his one and only Son" (John 3:16 NIV), and Jesus' best gift was also giving because Jesus "gave Himself [as a sacrifice to atone] for our sins" (Galatians 1:4 AMP). Before you married, you were both excellent *givers*, and that benevolent attitude led you to the altar. Just like your premarital days, your marriage will only work when both of you work at being *givers*. Satisfying marriages have two consistent *givers*! And the best way *to prove your love is through giving!*

On the other hand, sinful *selfishness* destroys the happiness connection and wrecks satisfaction for almost every couple. The Bible declares, "For where jealousy and selfish ambition exist, there is disorder [unrest, rebellion] and every evil thing and morally degrading practice" (James 3:16 AMP). If either of you are always looking out for "number one," your marriage will struggle. If your primary goal is to love yourself, you will become lost in loving your spouse. Being self-centered rather than other-centered is destructive. Selfishness is a destructive personal problem that is similar to narcissism and has demolished many marriages. In fact, I have never seen one happy marriage when one spouse is selfish.

I have heard numerous statements regarding selfishness: "My husband is extremely selfish and does exactly as he wishes." "Our marriage is all about what my wife wants, and we always do things her way. She is extremely selfish, pouting, moping around, and then acting like a little girl when she doesn't get her way." "Before I married my wife, her dad urged me to take a leadership role with my wife, by putting my foot down and establishing healthy habits. Otherwise, he said, I would reinforce her selfishness and she would want to be spoiled. Now, I only have regrets." "We are not in our marriage together because the relationship is all about my husband's wishes." And finally, "With every aspect of our marriage, as long as she gets what she wants; then she is kind, nice, and everything is fine."

In order to have a satisfying, rewarding marriage, both of you must be selfless in your relationship because time equals love! To learn if you are more selfless or selfish, simply evaluate your time. Assess how you spend time with activities, others, your spouse as well as your personal time. A key question is this: "How do I use my time to build up our marital relationship and serve my spouse?"

On the other hand, it is extremely selfish to place demands upon the majority of your spouse's time and to seek to control nearly every minute of their life. As covered in Lesson 60, self-time and home-time are important for every happy marriage. Thus, what we expect of our spouse's time can also help us evaluate our selflessness or selfishness.

The Bible encourages, "Do nothing from selfish ambition or conceit, but in humility count others more significant than yourselves" (Philippians 2:3 ESV). Personal happiness in life comes from being selfless. Likewise, marital satisfaction comes from both of you being selfless, not selfish!

Whenever you focus on others, including your spouse, you become less consumed with yourself, and your marriage is more likely to prosper. As Philippians 2:4 encourages, "Let each of you look not only to his own interests, but also to the interests of others" (ESV). However, if your focus is on keeping your spouse happy just to prevent turbulent times, you are really not being selfless, but instead you are living with a high-maintenance partner and only striving to keep the peace in order to survive a troubled relationship.

When you are dissatisfied with your spouse and relationship, the temptation is to ask, "What am I *getting* from my spouse and our marital relationship?" WRONG QUESTION! The essential question must always be, "What am I *giving* to my spouse and our marriage?" When both of you are acting like Jesus, desiring to be a servant to your spouse rather than be served, your marital satisfaction automatically increases.

After a few years of marriage, the *giving* aspect that dominates behavior before marriage may start to slip away. Such complacency will create many negative habits, including a lack of regular *positive giving* to your spouse. If you are giving anger, selfishness, or criticism, in all likelihood you are receiving that in return from your spouse.

To overcome selfishness, strive to be like Jesus and implement the attributes of *compassion, humility*, and *service*. Matthew 14:14 declares, "When Jesus landed and saw a large crowd, he had *compassion* on them and healed their sick" (NIV). Contained in the word *compassion* is the word *passion*. Have a passion for ongoing compassion toward your spouse.

One hurting wife said, "My husband thinks he is always right and better than me," indicating a lack of humility. A happy marriage will have two *humble* spouses, with an attitude similar to the humility Jesus possessed. Philippians 2:8 states, "And being found in appearance as a man, he humbled himself by becoming obedient to death—even death on a cross" (NIV). Imitate Christ's *humility* and think more of your spouse by thinking of yourself less. In addition, seek every opportunity to *serve* your spouse just as Jesus served mankind through His suffering and death on the cross. Matthew 20:28 says, "The Son of Man (Jesus) did not come to be served, but to serve, and to give his life as a ransom for many" (NIV).

Love is being most concerned about your spouse's well-being, not your own! Love is continually seeking the very best for your spouse every day! After God, your spouse is your number-one priority, not yourself! Ask, "What do I sacrifice for strengthening our marriage and building up my spouse?" Selfless love is a tall order for anyone. Give love freely without waiting for a reward. Have a *servant-attitude* without waiting to be served. Like Jesus, *compassion, humility*, and a *servant-like spirit* create a selfless spouse. And your true character always shows up within your home, not outside your house.

In all areas of your relationship, your *compassion*, *humility* and *service toward your spouse* will indicate how selfless or selfish you are. To avoid being selfish, go way past the line of saying and doing what is fair through self-sacrifice. By trying to out-serve your spouse, you automatically create a positive marital connection. When your number-one priority is encouraging and nurturing your spouse, your *servant heart* will significantly diminish selfishness.

Since your marriage is a partnership, both of you must make your relationship a priority in order to have a satisfying marriage. Both of you should make it a goal to give each other as much pleasure as possible while being committed to minimizing one another's pain. Being second is not easy, but by giving and daily demonstrating loving actions, you reinforce your marital commitment.

Generosity is one of the best attributes you can possess. Two generous spouses give continually with affection, appreciation, forgiveness, cooperation, sexual intimacy, household tasks, etc. A satisfying marriage has two spouses *giving* 100 percent because both recognize a rewarding relationship is the result of two people working hard every day to become better and better at giving to one another. It takes two *giving* spouses to make a healthy marriage, but only one unhealthy or *taking* spouse to break it.

Another challenge may be learning to take or receive gifts from words and actions. Due to low self-worth, some spouses struggle receiving behavioral gifts or verbal appreciation. Always be willing to receive when your spouse wants to give through words or actions. In order for your relationship to be satisfying, it is very important to not just *give*, but also to *receive*, because a healthy balance is necessary. When you receive any type of gift from your spouse, simply say, "Thank you."

When both of you continually put each other first with a desire to please, your home will become an environment of encouragement. And when *both of you give 100 percent* and have a desire for growth, you almost guarantee a satisfying marriage. Only through constant *giving* to your partner will you feel better about yourself and marriage. Be a spousal *giver*, *NOT* a spousal *taker*!

48. NO OPPOSITE-SEX FRIENDSHIPS

Of all the marriages that I have seen end in divorce, I estimate that a third of the time an affair is the reason. Due to the newness and false passion that is experienced with an affair partner, the marital couple often has little chance of restoring the relationship.

God warns every spouse in Proverbs 4:23, "Watch over your heart with all diligence, for from it flow the springs of life" (AMP). All of our actions flow from our thoughts, and therefore, we must be on constant guard with our thoughts. Both emotional and physical affairs begin with our thoughts. Most spouses never have the intention of being unfaithful, not recognizing that affairs begin in the mind. No matter how godly a person may be, every spouse in the world is capable of unfaithfulness. As mentioned in Lesson 10, King David, a man "after God's own heart" (see Acts 13:22), had an adulterous relationship, revealing the weakness of the flesh when tempted by sin.

One sure way to put your marriage in danger is to have *close friends of the opposite sex*. Think of all your relationships like bank accounts. A rich, rewarding marriage has a positive balance because the deposits—nurturing words and behaviors—exceed the withdrawals—hurtful words and painful actions. However, with an opposite-sex friendship, there typically are only deposits, and rarely withdrawals, which can give it the illusion of being more attractive. Limit your *innocent deposits* with friends of the opposite sex because those credits quickly escalate. And when the friendship account balance exceeds the balance between husband and wife, the marriage is in danger of collapse.

Almost every adulterous relationship begins as an innocent friendship with a person at work, a neighbor, or even a fellow church member. In addition, affairs often commence through such seemingly harmless online activities as e-mail, text messaging, and social networking sites. I believe approximately 25 percent of affairs that I have seen began through some form of technology.

I estimate another half of the affairs I have seen began with a person at work. Unknowingly, daily talking and eye contact with coworkers may produce an "unhealthy friendship." One unfaithful spouse shared in counseling, "Our affair began so innocently, drinking coffee together in the morning, going to lunch, texting after work hours about business matters, and 'helping' each other by discussing our marital problems. Unintentionally, our feelings grew stronger with each work connection, progressing from frequent conversations, to kind compliments, to simple physical touch, to hand-holding, to hugs, to kisses, and eventually, to physical unfaithfulness." Another unfaithful partner told me, "My coworker gave me more compliments in one month than my spouse gave me during our twenty years of marriage." Thus, work when at work, and avoid temptation by not becoming close companions with coworkers of the opposite sex.

Am I saying that you must avoid all interaction with members of the opposite sex? Of course not! But without clear boundaries, know that *opposite-sex friendships* can quickly become entangling affairs. Frequent contact with a person of the opposite sex can often lead to a powerful emotional connection that grows into an eventual strong physical bond. And the process often happens subtly.

If you place a frog in boiling water, it will jump out. However, if you place a frog in lukewarm water and turn the water up to heat slowly, the frog will eventually be boiled to death without realizing it. Having a friend of the opposite sex is similar to placing a frog in lukewarm water. Stay in the water too long, and you may have no idea when you are about to be boiled.

A marriage is in jeopardy when partners don't perceive any risk in having close opposite-sex friendships. I have had spouses say that they can have friends of the opposite sex and they have no intention of ending or dialing back those relationships. If that is your thinking, I have one question: "Can you go to a casino and gamble day after day for five or six hours per day and be profitable?" On some days, you would lose in a major way because the percentages are against you. Likewise, you may be able to have friends of the opposite sex and never have an affair, but the odds are not in your favor, so why take the gambling chance?

Everyone is susceptible to sin, and it takes years to build trust, but even a brief fling can destroy it completely. Boundaries create a secure marriage. To prevent any possibility of an affair, clear limits are essential, such as restricting your individual friendships to those of the same sex and relating to people of the opposite sex only as a couple.

Talk with your partner to mutually establish reasonable limits with people of the opposite sex out of respect for each other and your marriage. By avoiding even minor or innocent deposits with *opposite-sex friends*, you will earn unwavering loyalty and faithfulness with your spouse, as well as prevent a devastating affair.

49. DON'T EXPECT AN *A+* OR EVEN AN *A* MARRIAGE

Please understand that gratifying relationships are not exempt from struggles. Like the stock market, every marriage will have its ups and downs. No relationship has ever been consistently satisfying on a daily basis. The very best a marriage or a spouse can ever be is an *A-*. To expect your spouse or marriage to be an

A+ or an *A* will only damage your perspective of your relationship, because those grades are unattainable.

In the Old Testament, the Bible declares, "Indeed, there is not a righteous man on earth who always does good and who never sins" (Ecclesiastes 7:20 AMP). In the book of Romans we read, "All have turned aside, together they have become useless; there is none who does good, no, not one" (3:12 AMP). One surefire way to feel frustration and disappointment is to "fantasize" about the perfect marriage and the perfect spouse. If either of you has that fantasy, you will continually be disappointed in each other. When you expect an *A*+ or an *A*, anything less simply turns out to be an *F*—a failure. You or your spouse will never be perfect like the Son of God, Jesus Christ. There never has been or ever will be the perfect marriage or a sinless spouse.

Lifelong marital happiness does not mean daily happiness, either, because that is an impossible dream for any couple. I encourage both of you to frequently say these statements to each other out loud: *"There are times when I will disappoint you,"* and *"There are times when you will disappoint me."* Memorize these statements and repeat them to each other often, especially during the tough times. ALWAYS strive for an *A*-, but realize that as an imperfect and sinful spouse you will never consistently be an *A*-. So lower your expectations for your marriage and your spouse.

Understand there is a difference between what you expect and what you strive for. I expect my wife to be a *B*- wife, but I absolutely believe she is striving to be an *A*- wife. I am expecting *Simple Habits for Marital Happiness* to be a *B*- book in helping your marriage, but I am striving to write an *A*- book.

I counseled a wife married twenty-three years who could not understand the importance of lowering her expectations. Her three best friends had all divorced their husbands, and she told me all three of them had since found *A*+ boyfriends. What she did not remember is that for premarital relationships as well as affairs, there is the untrue perception that the "ideal" or "perfect" mate has been found—a significant error in thinking that usually leads to unhappiness..

She had a really hard time understanding why her husband could not be an A+ husband like those A+ boyfriends. This wife of twenty-three years told me that if her husband could not daily be an A+ or even an A spouse, she wanted a divorce because the A+ guy was out there somewhere, waiting to be found. She set herself up for continual disappointment with her husband because there is not an A husband in the world.

I then asked about her mom's relationships. She said, "My mom expected my dad to be perfect." Her husband then chimed in and said, "Her dad out of frustration eventually just gave up trying to be perfect and divorced her mom." The wife went on to say that her mom experienced the same phenomenon in her second marriage with a second divorce. Now, at age seventy, her mom was still searching for that perfect A+ husband. This wife simply could not comprehend her major thinking error, a core belief that was a false truth.

Please realize that even when there are no children in the home, the best any marriage can be is still only an A-. When children are present, the best any marriage can achieve is a B and also realize that less than 5 percent of marriages achieve that. A B- marriage means that there are more good times than bad times, and that is truly healthy marital satisfaction.

In every satisfying, rewarding marriage, there are good times and there are not-so-good times. A very happy marital relationship with no children will be an A- most of the time, but disappointments are still inevitable, and those satisfying relationships will slide down to B- at those times. Through Christlike words and actions, and simple positive habits, an A- couple will move back up to an A- relationship. Likewise for a happy couple with children, a B- marriage will be present most of the time, but when hurts happen, the relationship could become a C- one until positive words and behaviors once again create a B- marriage.

Children require care; child care takes time and energy; and the time and energy devoted to child care means there is less available of each for the marriage. If you have children under your care and you believe your marriage is a C+ or a B-, I say, "*God bless you,*" because you actually do have a healthy relationship. If you have no children in your home and your marriage is an A-, again: "*God bless you.*" As a spouse, ALWAYS remember to personally STRIVE for A- but only EXPECT your partner and relationship to be a B-.

50. AVOID SARCASM

In the Greek language, the word for *sarcasm* means "tearing of flesh." The Bible says, "Some people like to make cutting remarks, but the words of the wise soothe and heal" (Proverbs 12:18 TLB), and Ephesians 4:29 says, "Do not let unwholesome [foul, profane, worthless, vulgar] words ever come out of your mouth, but only such speech as is good for building up others" (AMP). Throughout my years of helping couples, I have witnessed sarcasm damage and even destroy too many marriages. We can all be sarcastic, and at times sarcasm is humorous and not detrimental—but that is rare. Ninety percent of the time, sarcasm is meant as a putdown; it is attacking, destructive, and significantly painful.

Sarcasm can be defined as hidden anger. *Sarcasm* is a way of slightly cutting your spouse and then saying, "I didn't mean it." Unfortunately, a devastating sarcastic comment is often thought to be made in fun. But sarcasm is a lot like eating chocolate cake with vinegar on top. No matter how good the cake is, the vinegar will always make the cake taste horrible. So, *sarcasm* is usually a major putdown covered up with, "I am just trying to be humorous and lighthearted."

A sarcastic spouse will often tell their partner, "You are just too sensitive and can't take a joke." However, although a sarcastic spouse wants to appear fun-loving, they are really being unkind and inconsiderate. Sarcasm is an indirect way of coldly whacking your spouse. For example, a spouse will make a sarcastic comment about something really bothering them because of underlying anger toward their partner. Then, they will make the comment that it was only a joke and their spouse should not take it seriously. When you or your spouse makes a sarcastic comment, even if you say, "I was only teasing," that is still devaluing your spouse's character.

Sarcasm can also be demonstrated with a contemptuous smile or rolling one's eyes to invalidate your spouse. *Body language sarcasm* is just as devaluing as *verbal sarcasm*. *Body language sarcasm* can quickly destroy marital happiness. Whether the sarcasm is conveyed through body language or verbally, it is a way of going "over the top" with a reaction to belittle your spouse and then denying it by saying you were just joking.

You may be using sarcasm to express feelings of hurt and disappointment because you are not able to share those feelings directly with your spouse. By indirectly sharing heartache through sarcasm, you are hoping to avoid defensiveness and retaliation by your spouse. Instead of sarcasm, use the *speak the truth in love* formula covered in Lesson 38.

I counseled a couple whose son lacked motivation due to low self-worth. Mom and Dad admitted to being extremely sarcastic both with their son and each other. I asked them to totally cease the sarcasm with their son and even encouraged them to not be sarcastic with one another for the sake of their marriage. They agreed to no more sarcasm with their son but said that sarcasm was the way they enjoyed "jabbing" each other. For a second time, I cautioned them about sarcasm. What happened? Their son improved dramatically, but unfortunately their marriage deteriorated because they did not drop their sarcasm.

As I stated in an earlier lesson, laughter coupled with a sense of humor is absolutely essential for a rewarding marriage. However, sarcastic humor will eventually erode your marital foundation and destroy your emotional connection. Try going for one month without being sarcastic with each other and see how much your relationship improves. *Please* avoid ALL *negative sarcasm* with each other!

51. THE BEST GUARDS: IMPROVE YOURSELF AND NEVER COMPARE

As a spouse, *when you stop becoming better, your marriage stops becoming better*, and that usually starts a slide toward the disease of complacency and perhaps even marriage failure! Answer this key question: *In every area of your life and marriage, are you a better person and spouse today than the day you married?* If both of you answered "Yes," I can almost guarantee that your relationship is rewarding and happy. However, if either of you has not been striving for continual improvement, your marriage is probably stagnant, and you most likely are just coexisting as roommates. Never take your marriage or spouse for granted!

The Bible encourages us to grow spiritually, "Grow [spiritually mature] in the grace and knowledge of our Lord and Savior Jesus Christ" (2 Peter 3:18 AMP). Likewise in gratifying marriages, the *first guard is spousal growth*, which is a commitment to get better and better in every way as a spouse. So, the *first guard* is a strong yearning to *improve daily as a spouse*. A healthy spouse has an intense desire for positive development in all aspects of the relationship, so the marriage becomes better with each anniversary.

Physically, individuals who are healthy usually employ positive habits, both with well-balanced meals and exercise. Relationally, it is also absolutely true that happy couples put healthy habits into practice! The vital solution is to never be complacent by regularly examining your words and behaviors. Have a willingness to become better and better in all marital areas to create more satisfaction. You cannot change your spouse but only improve upon your words and actions. When you improve yourself as a spouse, you definitely increase the probabilities for a gratifying relationship. A constructive ripple effect occurs within your relationship when you focus on self-improvement, not spousal improvement.

A spouse who has almost no desire to improve will say something like, "I know that I am a lousy husband" or "I realize that I am a horrible wife." By playing the victim, such a spouse suggests, "Just tolerate my unhealthy behavior because I am too pathetic to make improvements." Such a perspective conveys the thought, "I will never be better than the day you married me." Sadly, your marriage will struggle if one of you improves and the other refuses to make any positive changes.

Too many times I have heard spouses tell their partner in a marital session, "When you married me, you knew my flaws and now you need to accept me because I have no plan to improve myself." One spouse in counseling even told me, "I can't think of anything I would like about being married to me." Unfortunately, this person had no desire for improvement and surprisingly was shocked when their spouse asked for a divorce. Another unhappy spouse told me, "My partner has absolutely no motivation for becoming a better spouse, and thus, improving our relationship."

A familiar bad habit is easier to maintain than to change. Yet those annoying habits will usually negatively affect your spouse. If one partner continually strives to grow and the other resists improvement, your marriage will flounder. Hence, any marriage will have trouble if one spouse is unwilling or unable to improve.

Daily, as a spouse you do not earn the same "grade"; you are either slightly better or slightly worse. Continually evaluate your qualities for ongoing strengthening and flaws for areas of self-improvement. Self-evaluation includes asking yourself several important questions: "What would I like about being married to myself?"; "What would I dislike about being married to myself?"; and "How much time do I devote daily to nurturing my spouse and giving to my marital relationship?" If either of you is unable to do a self-evaluation, the chances are heightened that your marital relationship will struggle.

Hence, saturate yourself with a "growth attitude." Give a good consistent daily effort in becoming the healthiest spouse you can be. Never become complacent with your faith walk, attitude, prayer life, encouragement, affection, hygiene, sexual intimacy, personal development, etc. What you and your spouse need to believe is, "As your partner, I have a strong aspiration to daily be a relationship student, a lifelong learner. Every day I will keep improving myself by strengthening my virtues and fixing my flaws."

You only have control over becoming the best spouse you can be. Both as a person and a spouse, every day in every way become better and better. You cannot change your spouse, but by reading this book you will become a better spouse and develop a stronger emotional connection in your marriage. Every successful marriage requires two partners who take responsibility for ongoing spousal development. Every fifth-year anniversary, look back on where you were five years earlier. However, do not be embarrassed at where you were as a person and a spouse at that time. Instead, be very proud of your efforts toward improvement and how much you have grown over those five years.

An important component for successful, rewarding relationships is two spouses seeking to overcome annoying habits. Thus, always focus on a daily A- effort to improve yourself! Both of you will then happily state, "We strongly desire to work hard and become healthier spouses." That type of effort will increase your self-esteem and self-confidence, thereby enhancing your marital relationship!

To one day celebrate your fiftieth wedding anniversary, strive for continual self-improvement. So, starting today, have a daily goal to become better and better in every way. Use the beneficial behaviors from *Simple Habits for Marital Happiness* to establish a commitment for lifelong growth. Constructive behavioral repetition creates healthy habits. Those pleasing habits will lead to a positive relationship with your spouse. *For long-term satisfaction, spousal growth is always mandatory! Daily, do your best and strive to be even better tomorrow.*

The second guard is to avoid comparisons. Don't compare yourself to your partner, other spouses, or your marriage to other couples. When you compare, there is the temptation to believe that you are the better person, the better spouse, or even have the superior marriage. Such a negative comparison leads to the sin of pride.

However, whenever you or almost anyone makes comparisons, the comparisons are usually "up" and not "down." That means you will compare yourself to others or relationships that are in some way better. The result is lower self-worth because you, your spouse, or your marriage does not measure up in that comparison. Then you feel even worse about your marital situation, and this creates a feeling of hopelessness. Comparison is a thief that will almost always steal your joy.

With the *best two guards*, ask three essential questions. First, "Do I have a daily goal to improve myself in every way as a spouse?" Second, "In order to place myself on a continual growth path, I will ask my partner on a regular basis, 'How could I have been a better spouse to you this week?'" And third, "Will I avoid all comparisons with my spouse and our marriage?"

Be determined to implement the two essential guards! First, for long-term satisfaction **spousal growth is always required!** And second, ***avoid comparisons to other spouses and other marriages,*** but regularly compare yourself to where you were five years ago both as a spouse and a couple.

52. AVOID CRITICISM AND NEVER GIVE UNSOLICITED ADVICE

A major predictor for marital unhappiness and even divorce is *criticism*. Proverbs 15:4 cautions, "Gentle words cause life and health; griping brings discouragement" (TLB) *Criticism* is simply griping, complaining, and ridiculing. When a spouse receives criticism, it often feels like a lecture or a reprimand from a parent. To be constantly criticized is very discouraging and invalidating for a spouse.

One criticized wife told me, "When I go home, I look for how to avoid conflict, how to behave so he won't correct or criticize me. I constantly fear that one of my evening activities will set him off. I cannot win peace." Unbelievably, another hurting spouse said, "I was even criticized for how I eat ice cream." Ongoing criticism will quickly break down your emotional connection. And most fights and arguments usually begin with a critical statement, a huge negative strike against future happiness.

I counseled a couple where the wife continually corrected and criticized her husband on almost everything, including how to put the trash liner in the kitchen trash can. The husband said, "Sometimes it does not matter what I do because it is always wrong." I suggested that for one week both of them avoid the "Cs"—meaning that neither would *criticize, complain, condemn,* or even *constructively correct* one another.

The husband quickly and happily agreed to my idea, adding, "Let's go two weeks—no, I would like three weeks—no, let's follow your suggestion for a month." His wife immediately responded that my idea was stupid and that she would continue to regularly criticize in order to "help improve" both her husband and children. Certainly, the wife had an untrue perception of what she deemed as helpful. The couple also had several dysfunctional adult children, and she refused any more marital therapy. The wife's incessant criticism was taking a toll on the husband emotionally and physically.

Critical spouses are often perfectionistic, believing that anything less than 100 percent is an *F*. Certainly, no couple ever achieves 100 percent, nor is any spouse ever an *A*+ spouse, but a critical partner believes it is their job to constantly correct to achieve that unattainable ideal. Sadly, I have found that most critical spouses are also extremely poor at giving the *appreciation vitamin* and a regular "Thank you," as mentioned in Lesson 19. Due to a lack of personal self-worth, a critical spouse feels better when being a "fault-finder" rather than a "good-finder." Thus, instead of building up their partner, critical mates prefer to attack. Contempt builds, resentment grows, hostile feelings fill the heart, and that may lead at a minimum to an emotional divorce.

One way to evaluate if you are critical is to assess how often you demonstrate "C" behaviors—*criticize, correct, condemn,* and *complain*. Critical spouses seem to frequently *correct* even small actions; *condemn* how a spouse uses their time; and *complain* about even very minor irritations. Sadly, a critical spouse believes the false truth that their job is to continually improve their partner and their marriage.

Finally, I am not suggesting that you cannot seek improvements in your partner, because that would build up resentment. However, when you are disappointed, use the *speak the truth in love* formula explained in Lesson 38. Then, in a loving manner, make sure you focus on behavior, not character, with your requested change, and use the "Habits That Keep the Bond of Peace" described in the next chapter.

Tied closely to criticism and another essential skill is the instruction to *NEVER give each other advice*, UNLESS the advice is *asked for* by your spouse. Do not let it be said about you, "My spouse is constantly giving me advice. It is like they have all the wisdom in life, and I have none." Giving hasty, unsolicited advice creates bitterness and hostility because a spouse often feels incompetent.

Men especially want to fix problems, but that is not healthy for your relationship. Before giving advice to your spouse, always ask the key question: *"Do you want my advice?"* When my own wife has disappointments in life and shares those feelings with me, I now have learned to ask the same question, *"Would you like my advice?"* Most often her answer is "No, I just want to express my feelings and have you listen."

The happiest couples wisely watch their words and avoid the toxic actions of **criticism** and **advice-giving**. Bottom line, *criticism* is a significant negative and perhaps the first predictor for unhappiness that may eventually lead to divorce. And *NEVER give advice* unless your spouse asks for your advice. Whenever you are tempted to fix your spouse with a wonderful solution, always ask first, *"Do you want my advice?"*

53. AVOID THE "Ms": MIND READING AND MEMORY MATCHING

You can never be certain what your spouse is thinking. However, a major hurt and disappointment for many couples is the belief that you can *mind-read* your spouse's thoughts. It is simply unhealthy to assume you know what is going on in your spouse's mind. *Mind reading* is extremely annoying because absolutely no one can read minds.

Mind reading can be hurtful because many times you will be totally wrong. And even worse, when you are correct with your mind reading, that can frustrate your spouse because you know what they are thinking. A marriage can also be damaged when one spouse actually expects their partner to be a mind reader.

I counseled a husband whose wife actually separated and moved to an apartment because he could not read her mind. The husband was out of town on a business trip and his wife called him distressed over a particular situation. The husband listened with empathy, expressed compassion toward her, and even asked what she wanted him to do. The wife had family support and told her husband she was just sharing her heartache. When the husband returned home from the business trip, the wife had already moved to an apartment. She was enormously angry that her husband did not immediately come home after the phone call. The wife actually told him, "You should have read my mind and known that I wanted you to instantly get in the car and come be with me. You (the husband) starve our relationship of emotional closeness." The wife refused to attend counseling until her husband learned to read her signals, meaning her mind. The wife also thought making her expectations known, Lesson 35, was a "ridiculous" communication concept.

When you do not communicate expectations with each other, you will usually have chaos in your relationship. Plus, that often leads to trying to read your spouse's mind since you do not know what is going on in their head. So regularly share your thoughts and feelings about your day, yourself, and your relationship. In addition, remember to regularly make your expectations known to avoid the trap of mind reading. Finally, always ask, "What are you thinking?" to avoid mind reading.

The second "M" that can damage your marriage is *memory matching.* I often counsel couples that are struggling for happiness simply because they are trying to assess who is accurate with the past and who has the best memory. Your memory is excellent and always the truth—*from your viewpoint!* Whenever you recall the past, your memory changes from the reality of what happened. Usually your memory will be tilted in the direction of what you most desire for an outcome. When necessary remind each other, "We have agreed to not memory match." Please be careful when revisiting the past with your spouse and simply don't *memory match!*

Avoid mind reading and *memory matching* at all costs because those negative behaviors can quickly diminish your relationship satisfaction.

54. AVOID ADDICTIONS AND COMPULSIONS

Addictions place tremendous stress upon a marital relationship. The Bible warns, "Wine is a mocker, strong drink a riotous brawler; and whoever is intoxicated by it is not wise" (Proverbs 20:1 AMP), and it encourages: "Be sober [well-balanced and self-disciplined], be alert and cautious at all times" (1 Peter 5:8 AMP). Addictions destabilize couples because the number-one priority is the powerful pleasure rather than bringing happiness to your spouse. As mentioned in previous lessons, "it takes two to make it and one to break it." *Addictions* or any unhealthy *compulsions*—like alcoholism, habitual use of technology, overspending, eating disorders, pornography, drugs, gambling, or abuse of prescription medications—negatively impact both a spouse and a marriage. Addictions may also create a tremendous financial burden on a marriage, leading to even more relational upheaval. A spouse with uncontrollable harmful habits becomes an almost-impossible partner in terms of personal and marital satisfaction.

If you find yourself saying, "I *have to*" for stress relief, you are at risk for an addiction. For example, "I *have to* shop when I am unhappy to fill a void," "I *have to* go to the casino," "I *have to* drink some alcohol to relax," "I *have to* play video games," "I *have to* spend money to make myself feel better," "I *have to* exercise," "I *have to* control my food intake," or the opposite: "I *have to* continually eat," etc.

When it comes to objective facts about the problem, addicts often have confused thinking and use poor judgment. Where there is smoke, there must be at least a small fire. An addict usually sees no smoke, much less a small fire, and maintains the addiction. Not facing the problem creates excessive tension, conflict, and resentment within the marriage.

Whether the concern is alcohol, gambling, overspending, or any other addiction, a first goal would be to take a two-month abstinence from the addictive behavior. The abstinence is not a failproof assessment, but it certainly can be an evaluative tool for helping an addict face a serious problem. This initial objective will probably be met with defensiveness and resistance, however.

There are four steps that will lead to eventual healing. The first step is to help the addict or compulsive spouse overcome a *denial stance* of even having a problem. Denial can be a terrible thing because avoidance of the issue maintains the destructive behavior. The more anxious or insecure a person is, the more denial will be a challenge.

The second step to address on the road to healing is *minimization*. When minimization is the issue, an admission of a problem exists, BUT the addict thinks it is minor and not that big of a deal. For example, I drink too much alcohol, but I only excessively drink on Friday and Saturday nights. Minimizers have dark-colored glasses and are unable to see the light with their issue.

The third step to tackle is *rationalization*. When a *have to* spouse rationalizes there is at least an understanding that a possible addiction or compulsion exists, but the excuse is usually to blame the addiction on life problems, such as job stress or even the marriage. A rationalizer provides numerous explanations for their unhealthy behavior. Thus, false justifications block any desire for improvement and all help is still avoided.

The final step and eventual goal is *acceptance* where there is both recognition and the admission that a compulsion or addiction is present. Hence, a commitment is finally made to definitely overcome the problem. *Addictions* or *compulsive behaviors* can send your marriage down the dreaded slope of awfulness, so the eventual acknowledgment of a problem by an addict is a reason for thanksgiving.

In conclusion, the goal of this lesson is to provide a quick understanding of the difficulties, not an intervention plan. Recognition and seeking assistance for recovery will be the greatest challenge. If necessary, seek outside professional help for support in resolving an extremely complex problem. Finally, praise God if this lesson is not necessary for improving your relationship.

55. CLOSELY WATCH YOUR RELATIONSHIPS

The clichés are true: "Like attracts like," and "birds of a feather flock together." The Bible encourages in Proverbs 13:20 (AMP): "He who walks [as a companion] with wise men will be wise, but the companions of [conceited, dull-witted] fools [are fools themselves and] will experience harm." Furthermore, "The righteous choose their friends carefully, but the way of the wicked leads them astray" (Proverbs 12:26 NIV). Finally, "Do not be deceived: 'Bad company corrupts good morals'" (1 Corinthians 15:33 AMP). Develop right relationships as a spouse and as a couple because relationships are vital in what you will become.

Whether they are family or friends, you are the average of the five people you come into regular contact with the most. Like a sponge, you absorb those five individuals' beliefs about life, marriage, faith, values, work ethic, spending habits, etc. Associating with unhealthy friends and family members can destroy your marriage in a heartbeat.

I can think of numerous examples in which unwholesome family members or friends have broken up a marriage. A husband became a friend with several alcoholics and then became an alcoholic himself. A wife associated with women who were unfaithful to their husbands and very soon ended up committing adultery. A husband spent all his time with extremely selfish people, which increased his self-centered lifestyle and his eventual abandonment of the marriage because he wanted more freedom.

Identify the five people you associate with most, either in personal contact or through technology, and then ask several questions: How is their Christian walk and prayer life? How godly are their present and past decisions? How healthy are their marriages and relationships? What are their healthy habits and unhealthy habits?

Next, based upon their overall lifestyle, character qualities, and decision-making, give each of those five individuals a grade from *A*- to *D*-. For example, if the five grades are: *D, C, B, D,* and *C,* then the best you will probably personally become is a *C,* because you will become the average of the five people you associate with the most.

A key question to ask is, "Do my five closest associates make me a better Christian man or woman, building up our marriage and making us a stronger couple, or do they tear down the rewarding relationship we are trying to build?" You must absolutely choose healthy family members and friends for your closest companions, those who by their presence will help you grow in your Christian behavior and solidify your marital relationship. It is virtually impossible to have a satisfying marriage when family members or friends damage your Christian walk.

On the other hand, godly family members or friends will help you become a stronger Christian spouse, thereby enhancing your marriage. To benefit your marriage, be careful when choosing your associations with family and friends. Surround yourselves with godly friends and responsible family members, because those strong, positive Christian relationships will enhance your marriage.

56. NEVER USE THE "S" AND "D" WORDS

Always picture yourself as permanently joined with your spouse for a lifetime. God affirmed, "So they are no longer two, but one flesh. Therefore, what God has joined together, let no one separate" (Matthew 19:6 AMP). You pledged your commitment for a lifelong union, so speaking the word *divorce* is never the answer. Do whatever it takes to reach your golden anniversary. Pray for strength and the passionate desire to be the best spouse you possibly can be as both of you commit to developing a successful marriage. Your pledge of commitment on your wedding day was only the beginning of your lifelong commitment process. Thus, never threaten or intimidate by saying out loud, "I want to *separate*," or "I want a *divorce*."

You may think the "S" and "D" words, but *NEVER* say them *OUT LOUD*. To say out loud the "S" and "D" words only places a negative seed in your brain that your marriage is on the road to failure. *Threatening divorce* is a relationship nuclear weapon— extremely dangerous! And the more often you threaten divorce, the more likely that will become your reality. On the other hand, keeping those words only in your mind reinforces your commitment to improve your relationship through the *Simple Habits*.

Repetitive threats with the "S" and "D" words erode the foundation of a strong, satisfying marriage. We often become what we picture in our minds, and if you are saying the "S" and "D" words, the picture becomes more vivid, which increases the likelihood of those two negatives taking place in reality. Persistent intimidation with those words also forces your spouse into a corner. Often, when your spouse feels trapped in a corner, they will fight back with a vengeance. Regrettably, one way to fight back is to take up the offer for *separation* or *divorce*.

Even when a marriage is severely broken, I do not encourage separation. The odds of divorce increase to about 80 percent when couples live apart, so separation needs to be a decision of last resort. The only time I suggest a physical separation is when there is either physical abuse or extreme verbal abuse. Absence does not make the heart grow fonder, but a lack of physical presence does make the heart grow colder.

Rather than separate, have no sexual contact and sleep in separate rooms. Staying together under the same roof in a simple platonic relationship provides each of you with a daily opportunity to demonstrate Christlike words and actions toward each other. Such an arrangement also grants you the opportunity to daily read together *Simple Habits for Marital Happiness* to restore your relationship.

Bottom line: AVOID the "S" and "D" words! If *separation* ever becomes a reality, hopefully both of you are still willing to work for improvement by implementing the behaviors suggested in this book. Always believe in your marriage and your lifelong commitment to each other to eliminate any risk of failure.

57. BALANCE HOUSEHOLD ROLES

Both outside and inside *household roles* need to be accomplished for the smooth functioning of your marriage. Certainly, it is a falsehood that husbands only handle the outside household roles and wives are only responsible for inside-the-home tasks. For the sake of marital happiness, I hope neither one of you feel, "My spouse has no idea how imbalanced the roles are within our marriage." In order to enhance your marital satisfaction, a challenging, yet major goal is for both of you to clearly evaluate how balanced the roles are for your relationship.

I had one spouse tell me, "We have a very unequal partnership, just a huge imbalance. I have to do nearly everything to make our marriage work." I counseled another wife who did more than 90 percent of all the household tasks—mowing, snow shoveling, cleaning, cooking meals, household finances, getting the mail, taking the trash to the curb—nearly everything. Her husband believed his only role was to go to work and his wife was basically to be his servant. The wife told me, "Either I seek a divorce or continue living a horrible existence as an indentured servant."

A husband married for thirty years told me, "Rarely does my wife do anything around the house. Her dad had a miserable marriage because he did everything, and his wife, my mother-in-law, did virtually nothing. Her dad strongly encouraged me to expect my wife to do at least 45 percent of the household tasks or he said I would create a demon. I did not heed his advice, thus creating a broken relationship from our wedding day by doing too much for my 'princess'."

As stated in an earlier lesson, both of you need to be *givers*, BUT that does not mean you should be a slave and treat your spouse as a "princess" or a "prince" by handling the majority of all household functions yourself. Instead, it is important that a balance of household responsibilities is present within your relationship. Forget equality and *focus on fairness* with household duties. In a healthy marriage, the household responsibilities are somewhat evenly divided between 45 and 55 percent. An exception would be if your spouse is not capable physically or mentally to carry out even minor tasks.

Intentionally organize household responsibilities and have spousal goals. I have a sheet that I share with spouses listing about thirty inside and twenty outside household tasks. Perhaps both of you would gain a clearer understanding by sitting down and making your own list of all of the household tasks present within your marriage—balancing the checkbook, paying the bills, working outside the home, cooking meals, cleaning up after meals, vacuuming, mowing, handling medical expenses, weekly grocery shopping, etc. Hopefully, a written list of ALL your marital duties will make it easier to fairly divide the list.

Then, together write down what various household tasks, both inside and outside, each of you handle for the sake of a satisfying relationship. Keep in mind that some tasks take longer than others. Certainly, I am not suggesting a competition. Again, even in happy marriages, it will not be exactly 50/50, but a fairly equitable workload is important to prevent frustration and resentment from building up.

In addition, you may have a marriage in which one of you is the stay-at-home spouse. By "stay-at-home spouse," I mean that your "job" is in the home most of the day. Logically, you will probably do a higher percentage of the household tasks, maybe even 80 percent or more because your partner is already working forty to sixty hours per week outside the home. Both of you need to do your fair share so that one of you is not working many more hours in a week than the other one. An essential question is "How would I feel if we switched tasks and responsibilities for one week?" The best way to evaluate and even answer that question is to take on your spouse's tasks for one week.

If you were to reverse *household roles* and both of you are still happy, great! However, if your marriage has an imbalance with household tasks, it is absolutely essential to begin making specific expectations about what both of you need to do in order to create more balance in your household responsibilities. On a regular basis, as a friendly reminder, make a *"will you please"* request when household tasks are not being accomplished. The sooner both of you begin equally to share your regular household tasks and marital responsibilities, the better your relationship satisfaction will be!

58. GUIDELINES FOR IN-LAW RELATIONSHPS

In-law guidelines can produce family peace which helps create marital harmony. One very important idea is to always "CPR" your interactions with your in-laws. Every time you visit with your in-laws, be *civil*, *polite*, and *respectful*—"CPR." When conversing with friends or even acquaintances, you almost always

"CPR" those conversations. Likewise, implement that same consideration with your in-laws.

Think of your family relationships in the same way you think of your non-family relationships. Generally speaking, there are four types of relationships: 1) acquaintances, 2) friends, 3) "good" friends, and 4) "close" friends. Initially, your "new" relatives will probably fall under either category one or two. Do not expect to immediately become "good" or "close" with your in-laws but do lower your expectations in order to be relaxed during your visits with them. Hopefully, over the years, your relatives will become "good" friends, or better yet, "close" friends through regular, ongoing positive interactions.

Whenever a parent-adult child issue arises, the natural adult child should discuss the issue with their natural parents. Problems are usually created if you try to discuss hurts with your in-law parents. Frequently, when issues are discussed with in-law parents, the result is often a negative outcome.

As mentioned in Lesson 62, "Avoid Helpers," do not vent to your parents about your marriage struggles. And do not seek their advice unless you have first asked your spouse about requesting your parents' input. For example, maybe the two of you are planning to purchase a refrigerator and your dad sells refrigerators at a department store. Certainly, he has expertise with refrigerators, but you should still ask your spouse first if they mind you seeking your dad's input on the best refrigerator for your situation.

Tied closely to this guideline is for parents to never give unsolicited advice. It is a great temptation for parents to offer adult children advice when, in their viewpoint, things do not look healthy. Personally, it is hard for me as both a pastor and a counselor to bite my tongue when I have a concern, because I want the very best for our sons and their families. However, except in extreme circumstances, your parents must consistently abide by the "rule" to never give advice unless, as a couple, you ask for their advice. If your parents feel strongly about a concern, they should generally ask, "Would you like some advice?"

Another major area of importance is negotiation over holidays throughout the year. *Never monopolize one or more holidays!* In one troubled marriage, a hurting spouse said, "We never spend time with my family on Christmas Day and Thanksgiving Day. My spouse's parents are selfish and always get both holidays." A simple solution is to just alternate every holiday. Thus, if one set of parents has Christmas this year, the next year it will be the other parents' turn for Christmas. The same goal would apply for all major holidays.

A key question to ask is: "Would I be happy if we **reversed** how we now handle a certain holiday?" If either of you answers "No," then your holiday situation is probably not fair, resulting in marital dissatisfaction and hurt for one family. Hence, try to be reasonable in the amount of holiday time you spend with both families. Being equal with your time is almost impossible, but depending on the situation, hopefully the amount of holiday time will be fairly evenly distributed between families.

Your marriage may also have problems when parents come to your home unannounced. It is a good practice for parents to give advance notice and ask for permission first. However, if you want your parents to have the option to drop in on a whim, make sure both of you are in agreement on this policy.

In addition, it is usually not healthy for parents to visit with you for more than one week. If parents stay longer than a week, they are not just visiting, but instead "living" with you. Yet, if both of you mutually agree that your parents may stay as long as they want, that is your decision. Please realize the chances are slim that this will result in marital harmony.

Finally, never make negative comparisons about each other's family members. Of course, avoiding harmful comments is easier said than done, but still it is an essential guideline. Don't say "You are just like your dad/mom" unless it is a positive comment. For example, "You are just like your mom—an excellent cook who makes wonderful dinners each night." Or "You are just like your dad—with such a positive attitude." Unfortunately, most of the time when comments are made about in-laws, the statements are damaging and place a wedge between the two of you. A better approach when you do not like a certain behavior is to focus on a solution for that disappointing behavior, rather than telling your spouse, "You are like your parent."

Certainly, healthy parents can be encouraging, supportive, and help enhance your relationship. However, unhealthy parents can also create strife and tension within your marriage. For a positive parent relationship, please review Lesson 41 regarding "Leave and Cleave," as well as implement the guidelines from this lesson.

59. NO SILENCE

The Bible states that *silence* can be a virtuous attribute: "Even a [callous, arrogant] fool, when he keeps silent, is considered wise; when he closes his lips he is regarded as sensible (prudent, discreet) and a man of understanding" (Proverbs 17:28 AMP). However, *lengthy silence* can be an *emotional weapon*, with the goal of punishing one's spouse. Silence is actually the loudest form of shouting; it can frustrate a spouse and damage your relationship! Silence is actually worse than screaming at your spouse. Yelling, although tremendously harmful, allows for at least an understanding of the hurts and disappointments. Whether silence or yelling, both are significantly detrimental for your marriage.

Too many marriages have actually died due to the nothingness of silence. The *silent treatment* is not only frustrating, but it cuts like a knife and is just as harsh as a verbal tirade. A passive-aggressive spouse will use silence as a manipulative weapon because it is a form of control. The silent treatment often causes the other spouse to walk on eggshells. While healthy communication builds up a marriage, *aggressive silence* only tears down a relationship.

Remember the guidance in Proverbs 17:28: When your underlying intention is to avoid yelling and not overreact to a situation, silence may be beneficial for your marriage. But silence is only valuable when it is brief, less than an hour or, at the very most, no more than twelve hours.

A wife I counseled provides an example of harmful silence. She readied their three children for church while her husband stayed in bed and did nothing to assist her. Over the thirty minutes leading up to her preparing to leave, she asked him four times if he was going with her and their children to church. TOTAL SILENCE! He did not even say a quick "Yes" or "No." Eventually, she did what was healthy and left without him.

When she returned home, he screamed for fifteen minutes about her "rude, uncaring, selfish" behavior because she left without him. He also called her a number of negative names in front of the kids. She shared with him that his silence provided no clues for his desires. This troubled husband both verbally yelled and silently screamed. Unfortunately, the husband was not willing to change, and his frustrated wife eventually filed for divorce.

Sadly, I could provide numerous other examples of silence damaging marital satisfaction, often leading to divorce court. Silence only complicates marital problems and often causes love to die in the nothingness of recurrent silence. I remember a wife excusing her silence by stating, "My mom would sometimes not speak one word to my dad for thirty days," while she reported only withholding words for three to four days with her husband. Their relationship ended in divorce because she believed three to four days of silence was totally fine and she absolutely refused to stop her *silent screaming.*

Silence is truly the worst form of passive-aggressive behavior. Silence is hurtful communication, dishonoring to your spouse, and can inflict deep wounds on your marriage. If you have been guilty of giving your spouse the silent treatment, start by communicating through written words. E-mail, text, or provide a handwritten note, but please let your spouse know what you are feeling and thinking so they know how to meet your wants and needs.

NEVER devalue your spouse by "screaming and yelling" at them through the *weapon of silence*. In the chapter on the Bond of Peace. I provide a number of guidelines to help with sharing your hurts and disappointments in order to prevent silence.

60. SELF-TIME AND HOME-TIME GUIDELINES

God's goal for your marriage is oneness, or togetherness. However, doing everything together all of the time is simply not healthy for you personally, nor is it for your relationship. Eating chocolate cake is delightful, but devouring that cake three meals per day, seven days a week, would be sickeningly sweet. Happy couples take *self-time* for recharging in order to keep their marriage strong. Solo time allows for separateness, so that togetherness is even more meaningful. The Bible urges, "There is a season (a time appointed) for everything and a time for every delight and event or purpose under heaven" (Ecclesiastes 3:1 AMP).

My definition of *self-time* is doing something enjoyable outside your home. Self-time is absolutely essential for every spouse. The goal of self-time is to help you stay emotionally strengthened as a person, so you can become an even healthier spouse. Self-time never involves responsibilities such as grocery shopping, picking up the dry cleaning, etc. A lack of self-time often leads to emotional struggles and even can diminish satisfaction with your marital relationship.

Plan for *self-time* on a weekly or biweekly basis in order to recharge yourself and have a balanced life. Two suggested guidelines are: 1) Perhaps have self-time from Monday through Thursday to allow for together time on the weekends; and

2) NEVER be selfish with your self-time by spending more time away from your spouse than at home. Ideally, if each of you takes one day per week for self-time, that allows for five days of togetherness to connect emotionally.

Generally, your *self-time* will be a couple of hours and not more than two days per week. When you have self-time in the evening, make it a goal to be home at a reasonable time of night. Rarely should you stay out past bedtime because that may cause resentment, and it does not permit you to at least say, "*Good night, I love you,*" an *essential* from Lesson 22.

In addition, be considerate by *planning* for *self-time* rather than asking to do something on the day of an event. You are being considerate when you allow your spouse time to consider their schedule. So usually ask at least a few days in advance for self-time. A spur-of-the-moment request does not allow your spouse to say "No" without feeling embarrassed or guilty. In addition, to request self-time the same day is a rude way of basically saying, "I am going to put you on the spot and not give you a chance to say no. If you say no, I can make you feel guilty and tell others that you are a selfish person by denying me self-time."

Some activities that could be pursued during self-time include: exercising twice per week at your fitness center, going to a Bible study one night per week, or pursuing a hobby once a week.

Both of you also need *home-time* for recharging yourselves. My definition of home-time is relaxing within your house on a daily basis, by *doing whatever you want*. I am a little reluctant to suggest home-time, because some spouses are at the other end of the continuum and rarely accomplish anything. Thus, the goal is a healthy balance between being constantly on the go and being a couch potato.

I frequently hear, "My spouse is constantly on the go with no 'off' switch, finding it hard to decompress. We either have to be accomplishing chores or projects around our house, or we do some activity together away from our house. The word *relax* is not within our relationship." By always keeping busy, an "on-the-go" spouse gives the impression that "I am a special, active person, and you cannot justifiably complain." A spouse with a preoccupation for busyness will exhaust a partner and wear out a marriage. Even more detrimental, constant busyness will prevent emotional and physical intimacy.

I often ask an "on-the-go" spouse to sit and do nothing for just thirty minutes by reading a book or even watching television. The most common mistaken response is: "We have too many projects to complete or activities to attend." Relaxation is just not part of their vocabulary. The partner of a constantly "on-the-go" spouse usually feels guilty for wanting to relax and watch a sports game or a television show, or participate in a hobby. A constantly "on-the-go" spouse is frequently controlling and will not allow their partner any downtime. As a reminder, I described the *control fanatic* in Lesson 44. Within the home, the goal is for both of you to do whatever you want for a certain period of time each day.

For a satisfying marriage, *self-time* and *home-time* are both essential. As with most areas of life, a healthy balance between self-time and home-time is the objective. A key question is: How often do you have self-time and home-time? If your answer is "rarely" or "not often enough," you are probably feeling drained and your marriage is experiencing strain. Begin immediately to schedule *self-time* outside the home and recharge with daily *home-time*.

61. AVOID THREE "3-LETTER" WORDS

Three dirty "3-letter" words can destroy a marriage in a heartbeat. Never use the word weapons of *but*, *why*, and *you*. This is simply practical wisdom.

The word *but* is an eraser, a counter to what was said before the *but*. For example, "I love you *but* . . ." Or, "You are a nice

Christian *but . . .* " No matter what follows, the other spouse feels devalued and will not believe what was said first. In your home and marriage, I would encourage you to have poor grammar with run-on sentences by using the word "and." For example, "I like what you said *and . . .*" or "I think you are caring *and . . .*"

The word *why* attacks and places a spouse on the defensive. Using *why* does not look for answers, but only places blame and indicates that something is wrong. *Why* is an aggressive word that questions your spouse's motives and may create defensiveness. One spouse told me, "I hate the word 'Why' because it makes me feel I am always wrong." Much better to substitute, "*What are the reasons?*" or "*Tell me more about your motives*" for "Why?" because this indicates a search for understanding and solutions, not blame. For example, "**What are the reasons** you want to serve on the board at church?" rather than "*Why* do you want to serve on the board?"

Finally, the word *you* is only valuable when you encourage your spouse, for example, when you say, "You are a wonderful partner." However, when a sentence begins with *you*, it is often accusatory and puts your spouse on the defensive. In Lesson 38 you learned the *speak the truth in love* formula and the appropriate use of an "I Message." Reread Lesson 38 and always use an "I Message" rather than a *you* attack.

In summary, to enhance your relationship, avoid *but*, *why*, and *you*. Instead, begin now using "***and***," "**what are the reasons**," and begin sentences with the pronoun "***I***."

62. AVOID HELPERS

Talking to *helpers*—friends, family members, coworkers, neighbors, church members—about your marital disappointments is simply detrimental and potentially destructive. Whenever you talk about your spouse to any non-trained person, your relationship is often damaged. Remember how Job's friends mistakenly were of no help, and they even "condemned Job *and* declared him to be in the wrong [and responsible for his own afflictions]" (Job 32:3 AMP). Unintentionally, *helpers* can often become "breakers" of your relationship without realizing they are doing so.

Again, it is best not to seek advice and guidance from "helping" family or friends. For whatever reason, I have found that spouses who do seek advice from *helpers*, usually select those who do not presently or in the past have gratifying relationships. The bitterness resulting from a broken relationship often causes those types of helpers to have a negative view of marriage rather than an optimistic view. Thus, those *helpers* end up hurting a marriage a lot more than providing assistance.

Several other negatives occur if you decide to talk with an outside individual about your marital heartache. First, you are sharing only your perspective and they are not getting the full picture. Second, rarely will they counter your ideas because they are fond of you and do not want to hurt your feelings. Third, if you are discussing your marital concerns with a friend of the opposite sex, that might lead to an emotional affair, and that strong connection increases the likelihood of a physical affair. Fourth, helpers may unintentionally place a wedge in your relationship. Fifth, when you discuss pain and frustration with a family member, especially your parents, extreme discomfort will be felt by your spouse and family members whenever you spend time together. Family members may also end up taking your side, not the side of the marriage, leading to resentment and making reconciliation even more difficult.

You are "one flesh" in God's eyes, so always keep your problems just between the two of you. Whenever you have the urge to complain to someone else, don't do it! Instead, talk with your spouse about your concerns, and both of you look for solutions to the issues.

Whenever you are hurting in a marital relationship and you are unable to find a solution, I encourage you to talk to your pastor, priest, or a Christian counselor about your relationship. I also believe it is most beneficial to speak with a professional who has been married at a minimum the same number of years as the two of you. In addition, ask the professional for specifics on what they do on a daily, weekly, and monthly basis to improve their relationship and maintain constant growth for marital satisfaction. Find a counselor who focuses more on providing skills, like *Simple Habits*, rather than "he said, she said" dialogue so that you may gain the knowledge to resolve issues and build a stronger emotional bond.

63. CLOSE IT, PUT IT AWAY, CLEAN IT UP

Clutter can make it very difficult to be both internally happy as well as enjoy your married life together. Individuals with a cluttered home and/or car usually feel anxious and very chaotic on the inside. When a person has inner turmoil, they frequently have emotional problems and troubled relationships. In addition, clutter frequently creates resentment in the spouse trying to keep a fairly organized home and vehicle. However, I am not suggesting that your home and cars be perfectly clean, because that also can lead to problems. To have an organized home, follow the principle set forth in 2 Corinthians 8:11: "So finish what you began to do. Then your willingness will be matched by what you accomplish" (GW). To avoid a cluttered home, I strongly recommend an idea that has helped hundreds of individuals and marriages. I encourage you to type the following in large font, print it out, and then place it on your refrigerator:

<u>MARITAL RESPONSIBILITIES</u>

OPEN IT, CLOSE IT
MESS IT UP, CLEAN IT UP
GET IT OUT, PUT IT AWAY

For example, you get *out* the bread and peanut butter; *open* the peanut butter and make a sandwich; *close* the peanut butter and bread; *put away* the bread and peanut butter; and finally *clean up* the bread crumbs. Completing these tasks actually gives you energy as well as increases your self-worth. But most importantly, *closing it, cleaning it up,* and *putting it away* also helps your marriage, and your spouse will appreciate your thoughtfulness and consideration.

I also encourage you to apply the same principles to your cars. By keeping your car and home decluttered, you have a win-win both personally and for your marriage. Enhance your life and relationship by always *closing it, cleaning it up,* and *putting it away.*

CHAPTER VI

HABITS THAT KEEP THE
BOND OF PEACE

A common misconception is that if a couple regularly disagrees, they are headed toward divorce. Not true! Disagreements are natural occurrences in happy marriages. Couples in satisfying relationships certainly have disagreements—but they rarely have fights, arguments, and conflicts. The latter breaks bonds and places you on the brink of a deteriorating marital relationship. So, a disagreement is never the problem; it is how the two of you handle your disagreements while finding a solution that can make or break your marriage.

Healthy disagreements are actually essential for both of you to remain emotionally close. My definition of a healthy disagreement is demonstrating respect for your spouse's differing perspective over an issue while you "make every effort to keep . . . the bond of peace" (Ephesians 4:3 AMP). To keep the bond of peace, God declares, "get rid of your bitterness, hot tempers, anger, loud quarreling, cursing, and hatred" (Ephesians 4:31 GW). So, disagree, yes; but disrespect, no. Gratifying marriages are made up of two people who are capable of possessing two opposite opinions, having a mutually respectful discussion of their differing viewpoints, **and** finding a healthy middle ground for the sake of their marriage. Hence, winning is all about the *marriage winning*, not just one spouse winning over the other.

Couples that have frequent fights, arguments, and conflicts live in relationship pain. I define *fights* as akin to two third-graders hitting each other on the playground. *Arguments* are two people screaming and yelling at each other. *Conflicts* are two countries at war with one another. Are you at war with your spouse? Without a doubt, couples that turn to screaming matches rather than civil disagreements frequently possess a turbulent, troubled relationship.

If this describes you, rest assured that you are not alone. So why do so many couples have marital fights? Simply put, most couples have no idea of the behavioral guidelines for keeping issues at the disagreement level and preventing them from escalating. When discussing hurts, if both of you do not feel "safe," your relationship will probably struggle. This chapter will help you have a safe home for discussing disappointments. Finding solutions will become so much easier with these simple guidelines. I believe you will be pleasantly amazed that healthy discussions are achievable—and those respectful discussions will make a dramatic difference in your level of happiness! Pleasant disagreements actually lead to more conversation, creating more real closeness.

64. TWO DISCUSSION PRINCIPLES ARE ESSENTIAL: ESTABLISH GUIDELINES AND BE A WORLD-CLASS LISTENER

Happy couples regularly solve problems, so the better you address your disagreement process, the greater the likelihood for a gratifying marriage. In order to achieve the goal for respectful discussions, healthy couples have a specific strategy for keeping the peace. Hence, smart couples address their disagreements with *guidelines* that will actually help strengthen their relationship. Not so in unhealthy marriages.

Understand that a disagreement is never the problem, but instead how the two of you structure your disagreement discussions.

Almost every happy marriage possesses a strong framework for handling hurts and disappointments. Unfortunately, although the lessons suggested in this chapter are very practical, rarely are these *guidelines* known and utilized by most couples.

Thus, the very first principle for resolving marital heartache is to *establish guidelines* for how you will treat each other during a disagreement discussion. These behavioral lessons are healthy suggestions rather than rigid rules. When discussing hurts, if both of you do not feel "safe," your relationship will probably struggle. The main objective for *guidelines* is to help you feel secure and respected when sharing your feelings, thoughts, opinions, and solutions.

Hence, you increase the likelihood of a rewarding marriage when both of you have a behavioral plan for your disagreement discussions. So, either use the guidelines found in this chapter or develop your own, but your *first essential principle is to decide on a set of discussion guidelines.*

The second essential principle, and the most loving behavior you can demonstrate toward your spouse, is *listening.* The Bible encourages, "Everyone should be quick to listen" (James 1:19 GW). There is no greater skill to be learned than listening deeply to your spouse. With disagreement discussions, couples in unhappy marriages usually only listen to each other for five to ten seconds before interruptions, yelling, name-calling, etc., begin.

Happiness is all about what you let your spouse say, not what you say! *So, don't talk too much, and be brief!* The better you learn to listen, the better your disagreement discussions will be, and more importantly, the better your marital communication will be. *You listen your relationship into happiness and good health—you* **never talk** your marriage to satisfaction. So, work hard at becoming an Olympic gold medal listener!

How do you know if you are an Olympic gold medal listener? First and foremost, you understand that listening does NOT mean acceptance of the information. Thus, you listen with little defensiveness by digesting your spouse's comments without taking them personally. You understand your spouse is sharing their feelings, thoughts, and viewpoint. *So, it is only information!*

In addition, both of you probably will be emotional when discussing an issue. The cliché is true: "Looks can kill!" So, your gestures and body language can also intimidate your spouse. Thus, you want to listen well by communicating respect with sensitive, empathetic body language. Although it may be difficult, strive to have caring facial expressions and body language in order to reduce tension, thereby de-escalating potential arguments, fights, or conflicts. Your entire body language must manifest that it is "safe" for your spouse to share their innermost feelings and thoughts.

As mentioned in chapter 2, a *heart connection* occurs through focused eye contact and attentive listening. Casual eye-to-eye heart talks must happen on a regular basis; otherwise disagreement discussions will rarely go well because you are not accustomed to eye-to-eye connections. When your hearts are bonded together, almost all issues can be resolved. However, without a heart connection, having healthy disagreement discussions will be a major challenge and probably end up damaging your relationship.

In conclusion, one of the main qualities for a long-lasting, satisfying marriage will be your ability to work through differences by *listening extremely well.* Your problems can only be workable when you closely listen to each other's feelings, reasons, and solutions. Thus, the focus for disagreement discussions is a *"WE"* mentality, meaning ***We must listen** to each other—the second essential principle!*

65. STAY INSIDE THE "NINES"

Ecclesiastes 3:1 states that there is "a time for every matter under heaven" (ESV). Couples should discuss serious matters only *inside the nines*, from 9:00 a.m. to 9:00 p.m. After counseling over a thousand couples, rarely can I remember a couple sharing that they had a respectful, solution-focused discussion before 9:00 a.m. or after 9:00 p.m. The reason is that your emotions are most tender early in the morning and later in the evening. When emotions are worn thin, it's easy to slip into the blame game, where your conversation becomes ugly and destructive.

Before implementing *inside the nines*, hundreds of couples shared having huge arguments when a disagreement started after 9:00 p.m., went long into the morning hours, and ended with significant harsh words and a damaged relationship. Then, they woke up the next day irritated, bitter, and angry about what was said the previous night. Even more detrimental, they began the next day with significant resentment that often led to more yelling and screaming, or even worse, the silent treatment for several days.

Rarely, if ever, is there an issue that needs to be immediately addressed after 9:00 p.m., when you could just as easily wait for the next day. The same is true before 9:00 a.m., when feelings are just as sensitive. Early in the morning, many spouses struggle to be pleasant, much less have a serious discussion. No matter if it is early morning or late evening, possessing a positive attitude while conversing about a potentially explosive issue can be extremely difficult. Before 9:00 a.m. or after 9:00 p.m., attack is more likely the name of the game, not a solution-focused discussion.

I remember an attorney telling me that his wife wanted to have a major discussion at 6:30 in the morning. He reminded her of their agreement to use the *inside the nines guideline*. She responded, "I don't care that it is before 9:00 a.m." and pushed for the serious discussion. The attorney said, "Our heated, vicious conflict got really ugly fast, and it took us over a week to recover."

Bottom line: You should only have serious discussions between 9:00 a.m. and 9:00 p.m. If you have different work schedules, you may need to make minor adjustments to the *nines* guideline. Find a healthy window of time that works best for you to have a solution-focused conversation.

In summary, when you discuss issues *inside the nines*, you frequently are in a better disposition and much more willing to come to agreement on the topic of discussion. I am not trying to be too idealistic, but hundreds of couples have improved their relationship by following this one simple guideline. Numerous spouses have told me that the *inside the nines* guideline actually saved their marriage.

66. ALWAYS SIT

Jesus provides an example for the importance of sitting with the greatest sermon ever, the Sermon on the Mount. Matthew 5:1–2 affirms this: "When Jesus saw the crowds, He went up on the mountain; and when He was seated, His disciples came to Him. Then Jesus began to teach them" (AMP). We may assume that the disciples were also seated in order to be great listeners and learners.

During initial marital counseling sessions, numerous couples describe huge, yelling fights with name-calling and vicious attacks on each other's character. I always ask, "Were one or even both of you standing for the conflict?" Almost 100 percent of the time, the quick response is "Yes."

Rarely, if ever, has a couple reported having an excellent discussion when both spouses were standing. Standing is a power position that not only intimidates your spouse, but it makes focused listening extremely difficult. If you stand while addressing an issue, it is so very easy to yell and "turn up the volume." When attempting to resolve significant marital concerns, if you stand, that is almost a guarantee your discussion will escalate into a yelling argument.

Hence, a goal is to *always sit* down for major talks about hurts and disappointments. For years, I suggested that couples find just any comfortable location for their seated discussions. However, I now believe that couples benefit more from a *kitchen table* discussion, similar to the conference table.

In the business world, typically a meeting is scheduled where all participants sit around a conference table. Management understands that attentive listening and focusing on solutions would be more difficult if everyone just stood. With associates seated at a conference table, beneficial discussions may happen where options are suggested and successful resolutions are found. Surprisingly, while this principle readily pertains to work, *sitting* for serious discussions is rarely applied at home.

I also believe that you should *sit adjacent* to one another at the kitchen table. This will allow you to hold hands, listen better, be more respectful, and focus on finding solutions rather than accusations. Being close enough to hold hands will often enhance understanding and compassion for your spouse's perspective. Touch not only lowers blood pressure, but it may also decrease tension while discussing a concern.

Another benefit from sitting adjacent is avoiding direct eye-to-eye contact. When you are in a disagreement discussion, that is one time you might not want to have direct eye contact. By sitting adjacent, you are able to respectfully look away if tension arises. Yet, you can still look eye-to-eye when your conversation is not as stressful.

If you have children, the kitchen table may not provide enough privacy. If this is the case, find a secluded location, like your bedroom, the basement, or some other private area within your home. Or perhaps talk when kids are in their rooms or in bed, as long as you stay *inside the nines* (see Lesson 65).

Wherever the location you choose to sit, you both need to be confident that safe discussions will occur where you will be able to have eye contact, listen intently, avoid blame, and find solutions. *Always sit* is definitely one of my top-ten pieces of marital advice!

67. SOFT START-UP

Another absolutely essential guideline is having a *soft start-up* rather than a harsh beginning. The Bible also encourages, "A soft and gentle and thoughtful answer turns away wrath" (Proverbs 15:1 AMP). When you have an abrasive, attacking beginning, almost 100 percent of the time you will have a disastrous ending, and that is a major predictor for unhappiness and sadly often divorce. For a barbershop quartet competition, judges can make a fairly accurate score based upon the first few bars. Likewise, you can determine how your marital discussion will often end based upon your first few words.

One spouse told me, "When my partner gets mad, there is NO filter." If there is a harsh start for a serious discussion or even a conversation, it will usually end in the same fashion, cruelly. What are examples of attacking starts? "You always . . . ," "You never . . . ," "You are so stupid," "You are so dumb," or much worse phrases. Even saying to your spouse "I have a problem with . . ." is a dangerous way to address a hurt, because that phrase comes across as attacking. Don't even use the common phrase "We need to talk." What begins badly with each other will often end badly—including your marriage.

I believe the very best phrase for a *soft start-up* is "*I need your help.*" A husband said, "*I need your help* humbles me and at the same time makes me feel compassion for my spouse's hurt, thus blocking out my pride." A wife told me, "When I hear *I need your help*, I am much more ready to listen and discuss." Another husband said, "*I need your help* makes me more aware of not just my disappointment, but also my goal of finding a solution that will make our marriage even better." One wife said, "*I need your help* is disarming and has significantly enhanced our marriage relationship."

Since all of your serious talks will happen when you are seated, the only place for using *I need your help* is in the home. Upon hearing the words, "*I need your help*" both of you should decide if you want to have a discussion immediately or schedule the "talk" for another time by saying, "Now is not a good time." If the answer is "Yes let's discuss," *always sit* when having that conversation.

I am confident you want to be helpful when your spouse has a disappointment with words or behaviors that may be creating marital dissatisfaction. Hence, you want to be a healthy spouse by always implementing a soft start-up. A *soft start-up* frequently heightens more supportive feelings throughout the discussion process.

Beginning a disagreement discussion with "*I need your help*" will definitely boost the chances of resolving marital disappointment because you automatically increase careful listening behaviors. And most importantly, a *soft start-up* will improve the probabilities for a successful finish!

68. SCHEDULE DISCUSSIONS

When you experience a hurt or disappointment, you quickly think, "I don't want to go to bed sitting on those feelings, I want to have a discussion right now." You are unhappy, probably possessing an attitude of attack, not wanting to even think about solutions. Unfortunately, wanting a vicious assault is a normal thought, but such an attack usually leads to an explosive time for your relationship, creating a wedge between the two of you.

If you have arguments and fights often, the odds favor at least one of you having a short fuse. Short-fuse spouses are usually emotional and irrational, *not* logical and rational. If either of you are impatient and combative, willing to argue about "stupid stuff," your marriage will not be as satisfying as you desire. Although most issues in a marriage are not life-or-death requiring an immediate solution, unhealthy spouses often lack self-control and seek an immediate resolution to a problem. Patience is a very important virtue when planning a positive discussion time.

Spur-of-the-moment disagreement discussions usually become fights, arguments, or conflicts. Spouses often say, "I thought God said to not let the sun go down while I am still angry" (see Ephesians 4:26). True! And waiting till the next day, or better yet, the weekend, will help you keep your anger in check. Hashing out your disappointments at that very moment will probably lead to severe anger, and that anger will last all night into the morning.

The key question is, "How can I keep from getting angry if we do not discuss the issue immediately?" I have several suggestions to help you keep your emotions in check. Since the most powerful form of communication is written, one alternative is to type out an e-mail using the *speak the truth in love* formula and save it as a draft. If you are still hurting, you could send the e-mail the next day. Or write a note describing your disappointment, and if necessary, share your note the next day. When you write down what is bothering you, that will also allow you to observe how frequently you get upset over irritations within the relationship.

Self-control is a fruit of the Spirit mentioned in Galatians 5. Every healthy marriage has two spouses who do not overreact when they experience a disappointment or hurt. Having the self-discipline to wait for an important discussion is a significant quality both of you must possess. At a minimum, postpone disagreement discussions for at least a day. Postponing a discussion permits you to schedule a disagreement talk for a more advantageous time.

Planning for disagreement discussions allows you to calm yourself down and actually demonstrates love toward your spouse. We plan for birthday celebrations, graduation parties, vacations, family reunions, holiday gatherings, etc. Likewise, as a healthy couple when you have a significant disappointment or hurt, you will also want to plan for those serious talks. Planning a time for a disagreement discussion is an absolute essential!

Thus, beginning today, always *schedule your sensitive discussions*! Probably the best days for disagreement discussions are either Saturday or Sunday. Generally, weekend discussions will allow both of you to be fully rested, placing you in a better mood, rather than during the week when you are rushed and stressed.

69. START LOW, SPEAK SLOW, AND USE VOLUME TWO

You basically have two choices when you are upset. You can either speak *low and slow* or *loud and fast*. A loud voice grabs negative attention because it is generally intimidating and frightening for a spouse. Loud and fast usually leads to yelling, name-calling, character assassination, etc. And when you yell at each other, you only hear half of what is spoken. Frequently, the result with loud and fast is an argument, fight, or conflict.

God provides two significant suggestions for utilizing "warm words" in order to have a respectful disagreement discussion. Proverbs 15:1 states, "A soft voice turns away wrath," (ESV) and James 1:19 says to be "slow to speak" (AMP). When you speak quietly with *soft* and *slow* voices, you will usually listen more closely to each other. Smooth, soft, and slow words can lead to smooth and safe discussions.

I have had spouses state that in their family of origin, or even in their culture, loud and fast was the norm. Sadly, one wife told me and her husband loud and fast was the only way she could discuss an issue because it was ingrained in her. In almost every case, when a spouse took a similar stance as this wife, the marriage remained unhappy.

A *loud and fast* tone of voice is not only terrifying, but it creates an intimidation factor. With a raised voice, over 90 percent of the time the discussion escalates into tension, with a harsh ending. Thus, if you do not learn to respect each other by avoiding *loud and fast*, rarely, if ever, will you have a positive outcome with a solution for your disagreement discussion.

Hence, the manner in which you communicate frequently determines if you have a disagreement discussion or a major conflict. A *soft*, *low*, and *slow* tone of voice communicates understanding and respect. Generally, the most important parts of a musical piece are the beginning and the end. So most musical pieces start softly and slowly, which is also what you want for your disagreement discussions.

Three examples can illustrate the importance of *low and slow*. When speaking to a baby, you nurture that child by softening your tone with low and slow speech. You lovingly care for the baby by lowering your voice and using calm gestures. As mentioned earlier, you know that "looks can kill," so you also have a facial expression that communicates love, care, and nurture toward the baby. Likewise, you will be especially thoughtful and kind when you intentionally speak to your spouse just like you talk to a baby.

The second example is that of a first-year teacher versus an experienced teacher. When a classroom becomes loud and disruptive, often a first-year teacher will yell and rapidly state, "Class, sit quietly and do your work!" I know because that is how I handled my classroom as a first-year teacher. The unfortunate result is that the class almost always gets louder rather than quieter. An experienced teacher does just the opposite of many beginning teachers and speaks in a calm, low, soft, and slow voice, "Class, will you please be very quiet and finish your work?"

The third example is how a police officer handles a domestic violence situation. Frequently, when an officer arrives on the scene, both spouses are often speaking loud and fast with one another. Police officers have told me they are taught "verbal judo," meaning they almost whisper in a *low and slow* voice to defuse spouses screaming and raging at one another. One officer told me, "If I yell at a husband and wife, they hear only half of what I say. However, if I speak very quietly, they listen more closely, and both usually calm down. And the positive outcome is less violence."

Whenever there is a sensitive issue, it is absolutely essential that you avoid speaking loud and fast with each other. To speak *low and slow*, you must have self-control, which really means that you must have "mouth-control." When you speak *low and slow*, you are demonstrating compassion, and that provides an opportunity for a good discussion and hopefully a compromise and a resolution.

I suggest that you understand the five volumes at which we can speak. Volume five is yelling; volume four is how loud you would speak to be heard in a crowd; volume three is conversation volume; volume two is your GOAL—*low and slow*; and volume one is a whisper. When you have a topic to discuss that can easily escalate to an argument, you want to choose volume two, *low and slow*, just as God's Word suggests: being "slow to speak" and "quick to listen." When you want your spouse's full attention, almost *whisper*!

A *low and slow* approach also allows for planned comments, NOT reactive responses. A planned comment almost forces you to "pause, pause, pause" before speaking. Planned comments are more intentional, thoughtful, and solution-focused. A reactive response is often an impulsive, harmful reply that ends up being thoughtless and sometimes combative. *Low and slow* usually produces a "pausing mentality," which enhances disagreement discussions through planned comments.

Change is difficult for all of us, but you can break old habits and learn new ones. If you did not learn *low and slow* during your formative years, you will need to become comfortable feeling uncomfortable with *low and slow*, in order to allow for healthier discussions. Soft, planned responses are also more likely to win your spouse's heart.

Always demonstrate respect for your spouse with a quiet volume and a warm tone of voice. Increase the probabilities for a healthy discussion with a *low and slow* conversation style. Discussing *inside the nines* and *always sitting* at the kitchen table will help provide you the opportunity to speak just above a whisper—*low and slow*. Bottom line with every discussion: Your spouse will not really care what you said, but he or she will always remember how you made them feel during the discussion. Hence, have a goal to make your spouse feel valued and loved during every disagreement discussion.

70. PLEASANT MOOD

Satisfying marriages have two spouses who are pleasant, rational, and logical when discussing their disappointments. Spouses in an amiable mood are more likely to examine the facts and objective reasons for disappointments with a desire to understand what is best for the marriage. A commonsense spouse will also wait until they are in a pleasant mood before having a disagreement discussion.

Hence, if you are tired, hungry, irritable, or just plain not happy, having an *I need your help* discussion will usually end poorly, and thus damage your relationship. So, DO NOT have a discussion when either one of you is not in a good mood. On the other hand, when both of you are rested and content, you will have the energy to respond with respect to your spouse's *I need your help* concern. Always remember, harsh endings are a major predictor for unhappiness, separation, or divorce.

Many spouses ask me, "How do I handle all my pent-up frustrations even though I am not in a good mood but want to discuss things now?" A legitimate question is, "What is your goal: to destroy your spouse and drive a wedge in your relationship, or to find solutions for the words and/or actions that disappointed you?"

Most issues in your marriage are not "life and death" but can be handled the next day or even the next weekend *inside the nines*. As I mentioned in Lesson 68, if you can't wait until the scheduled discussion time, draft an email or write a note to your spouse using the *speak the truth in love* formula. The next day, assess if your email or note needs to be revised so it is "in love" and then share it with your spouse when appropriate.

God's Word has numerous warnings about harsh words for others, especially your spouse. Proverbs 15:1 tells us, "A gentle answer turns away wrath, but a harsh word stirs up anger" (NIV). Again, in Proverbs 30:33 (NIV), "stirring up anger produces strife" in your marriage. Thus, you should never have a serious discussion when you are tired, hungry, or unhappy. Most spouses exhibit agitation and irritability when they are exhausted or famished.

One significant idea to keep a respectful, pleasant mood is to picture a prominent house guest at the table with you—someone you deeply respect such as your pastor, children, grandchildren, a special friend, etc. Imagine that distinguished guest observing your facial expression, tone of voice, and body language. Picturing that person listening to you will often enhance your discussion.

To have a serious discussion without a good attitude and pleasant mood leads to more blame than solutions. Try to have a disagreement discussion after a meal, when you are likely to feel more content. A full stomach creates a calm mood and a stronger possibility for a respectful and rewarding resolution. Bottom line: Always wait until both of you are in a calm, content, and pleasant mood because you don't want to be embarrassed in front of your "distinguished guest."

71. USE THE RIFLE APPROACH, NOT THE SHOTGUN

Couples need to always address one solitary concern at a time, NOT several problems. To illustrate, a rifle has a single bullet, while a shotgun shell has numerous pellets. Couples need to take the *rifle approach* with *I need your help* discussions. When a crisis situation arises in a business, the management team will call a meeting and spend time focusing on one problem, NOT all the company's difficulties. Likewise, don't try to resolve all marital difficulties at once, just the present problem.

Too often, during disagreement discussions, troubled relationships jump from issue to issue, never resolve anything, and even worse, damage the marriage. If there are several concerns, schedule a disagreement discussion for another time, but always handle just one at a time. Thus, an essential key component for a satisfying marriage is a couple's ability to find a solution for just *one specific heartache at a time.*

When you have a hurt or a disappointment, you always want to take the *rifle approach* by focusing on a single concern, not numerous issues. If you take a shotgun plan of attack, issues rarely get resolved, and the result is often marital unhappiness. Be concise, state your concern in one sentence, and then focus on that one single hurt for a solution-focused outcome. Bottom line: Deal with only one *I need your help* topic at a time.

During the discussion, avoid bringing up painful incidents from ten, fifteen, thirty years before, or even longer. Troubled couples have a tendency to make past hurts part of nearly every disagreement discussion. I have heard it said numerous times: "My spouse will rehash hurts from years ago" simply to avoid resolving the present issue. Remember Lesson 9: Once a hurt is forgiven, let go of that past pain by not bringing it up to your spouse's memory.

In summary, when you have an *I need your help* discussion, always take the *rifle approach, not the shotgun approach.* If your concern is a major decision, perhaps use the decision-making process found in Lesson 45. In your marital disagreement discussions, always have the goal to simply deal with one stressor at a time and not attempt to fix everything immediately.

72. HAVE A DIALOGUE, NOT A MONOLOGUE

One of the primary reasons marriages sour is that one or both spouses have a single goal during disagreement discussions: to give a great *monologue*. A *monologue* is an unhealthy strategy to outtalk your spouse in order to win the discussion. On the other hand, one of the most loving behaviors you can demonstrate is to strive for a *dialogue*. So always dialogue your relationship to happiness, NEVER think you can monologue your marriage to satisfaction. The more the two of you *dialogue*, the more you will enhance your disagreement discussion.

Lecturing is for the classroom, and even that is not the best style for creating a learning environment; it usually is very frustrating for students. Talking too long indicates a lack of empathy and understanding for your spouse's perspective. By being brief, spouses avoid lecturing and encourage more of a dialogue than a monologue. The best marriage talks are always *dialogues NOT monologues.*

To cause "spousal deafness," speak in several paragraphs, or even worse, in pages, with your spouse. Your spouse will feel that you are talking AT them rather than WITH them. When you "lecture" or "monologue" *at* your spouse, one negative outcome is often withdrawal from future discussions.

Always have a *dialogue* by limiting your comments to three sentences or less. Share your thoughts in a short paragraph, NOT several paragraphs. Without a healthy dialogue, the communication process will often deteriorate.

Think of your *dialogue* like a tennis volley for exercise with your spouse. Your goal is not to competitively win a tennis match against your mate. Your goal is to experience exercise together, and in the process feel better about yourself and your relationship. Both of you would very nicely hit the ball directly at one another, attempting to keep each volley going as long as possible for better exercise.

Likewise, when you have a disagreement discussion, your goal is a nice ebb and flow of conversation balance between the two of you. If either of you just held the tennis ball and stopped the volley, one or both of you would walk off the tennis court, thus ending the enjoyable exercise or concluding the discussion.

Three major communication determinants for divorce are:

1. talking too much—having a monologue
2. a lack of listening
3. misinterpretations

One helpful way to deal with these problems is to *echo* back, word for word, what your spouse tells you and then *ask* if that is correct. Similar to a restaurant experience, after ordering your drinks, the server echoes back to you what you are asking for. Then, you order your meal and again the server echoes back to you your requests.

When you *echo*, word for word, what your spouse said, both of you are almost forced to maintain excellent eye contact. *Echoing* is also one of the best ways to ensure a dialogue. When you echo back to your partner, you also value your spouse through excellent listening. Listening well does not mean acceptance, but a desire to understand your spouse's perspective. Attentive listening and echoing encourage respect and understanding between the two of you, the foundation for a *dialogue*.

To *echo* back also avoids misinterpretations because you are trying to understand your spouse's viewpoint. Very simply, a healthy reflection would be something like, "I heard you say . . . Is that correct?" Healthy couples use some form of this *echo* technique.

Whoever brings the concern to the kitchen table will speak first, and the other person will listen. When you are speaking, you have the opportunity to share two thoughts. Your spouse would echo back each thought. Then, you give the "floor" to your spouse, and they share two thoughts and you echo those. Then, repeat the process. You can share just one thought if you like, but the goal is for each of you to have the opportunity to share a couple of thoughts for a nice ebb-and-flow discussion.

To increase the probability of a *dialogue* discussion, some couples have shared that initially they echoed only one sentence at a time. By sharing just one sentence and then having the other spouse echo that sentence, the entire process was more deliberate, creating a solid dialogue. Perhaps sit at the kitchen table and practice the *echo* skill with a light conversation topic in order to learn how to *dialogue* successfully.

73. SHARE YOUR OPINION

Your marriage becomes healthy when you do not have "a winner and a loser" in disagreements, but you establish acceptance and value by both of you feeling like winners. Being a winner is about allowing your spouse to express their viewpoint AND respecting their perspective. The ultimate goal for every disagreement discussion should be to understand your spouse's point of view.

Never express your feelings or thoughts as a fact or the objective truth when it is just your opinion. Your perspective will rarely be a fact. I counseled a man, divorced twice, who told me, "I was confident I could anger my ex-wives by telling them what I was saying was an absolute FACT, not just my perspective." Certainly, it was a fact that both his ex-wives could not tolerate his attitude and approach to discussions. It was also not surprising that both women divorced this man.

Another major mistake is trying to prove that you are right and that your spouse's opinion is wrong. Instead, your goal should be to understand the reasons for their perspective. Ask yourself, "What is going on within my spouse that would cause them to have that viewpoint on this issue?"

A husband stated in counseling, "With nearly every thought I share, my wife tells me, 'That is ridiculous.'" One wife told me, "There is not a lot of give-and-take because my opinion does not really matter." A husband shared, "My opinions only receive criticism and insults." One spouse told me, "I just don't share my perspective because my partner will make character assassinations. Then, we escalate into a full-scale war."

When you discuss an *I need your help* concern, a healthy approach is always to begin statements with one of the following: "My *opinion* is . . ." or "My *perspective* is . . ." or "My *viewpoint* is . . ." or "I *think* . . ." rather than stating something as the absolute truth that implies, "I am right, you are wrong."

You do not have to agree with your spouse's thoughts, but will you please always respect their perspective? You may eventually find that your spouse's point of view is just as good as your opinion.

In addition, please always take your *spouse's viewpoint* as information, not an attack. Let me repeat: **NEVER take the information personally!** Your marriage will struggle if either of you take opinions personally, because the outcome is usually defensiveness and retaliation. When you disagree over an *I need your help* concern, how do you respond? Do you stay agreeable and cooperative by searching for a solution, or do you strike back and attempt to get even because of your spouse's perspective?

Never attack your spouse as a person, but simply *share your opinion* about hurts over bothersome words and behaviors. When stating your *perspective*, you must absolutely never give your spouse negative labels. Negative labels only attack your spouse's character, which damages your marriage. Labeling is actually a way of attacking to avoid dealing with the issue. Understand that probably 80 percent of the time, when a spouse labels, it is that partner who really needs to make the most behavioral improvement.

You only win when both of you feel heard and respected. Thus, the goal of every discussion is to allow each other to *express opinions*. Please don't desire ever to suggest that your viewpoint is the total truth; instead, realize that a *perspective* is only an expression of inner feelings. When you respect one another's *opinion*, that develops trust and acceptance, eventually leading to compromise and healthy solutions.

74. UNDERSTAND YOUR SPOUSE WITH KEY QUESTIONS

With each disappointment, your main goal is to understand your spouse's perspective as well as their reasons for a particular hurt. When you understand your spouse's viewpoint, you enhance the chances of finding a solution to the hurt. To get to the facts, Jesus asked questions like, "How many loaves [of bread] do you have?" (Mark 8:5 AMP). Like Jesus, through questions you need to search for your spouse's viewpoint as well as reasons. Per Lesson 61, NEVER ask *why* questions! Instead, ask open-ended questions that begin with either *what* or *how*.

A disagreement discussion often turns into an argument, and a conflict happens because you do not understand your spouse's inner feelings. Thus, understand the reasons for your spouse's viewpoint with the *key questions*: "*What* are your REASONS for your position?" "*What* are your underlying concerns regarding this issue?" "*How* do you feel about my solution?" Seek first to understand not only your spouse's perspective, but most importantly, the reasons for their viewpoint. Feeling understood will often diminish the intensity of the disagreement.

When *open-ended questions* are asked, it is absolutely essential that both of you avoid being overly sensitive, because that usually leads to defensiveness. Overly sensitive spouses have their feelings easily hurt, and they thereby misinterpret even nonthreatening questions. For example, a husband said, "It makes no difference what questions I lovingly ask, my wife comes back strongly with a defensive attack. Thus, we never discuss and can't agree on anything." A wife shared, "I don't ask questions of my husband because there is no give-and-take—no compromise in search of a solution that meets both of our needs." If either of you are that delicate with questions, having a reasonable, commonsense discussion will be a challenge.

When you ask *open-ended questions*, you allow your spouse to express their feelings, reasons, and fears with every *I need your help* concern. So even if you don't fully agree with your spouse's position, you will fully understand their perspective, and that automatically increases the probabilities for compromise and an agreed-upon solution.

I encourage you to have a practice session asking questions regarding a lighthearted subject. For example, take turns discussing your dream two-week vacation if money were no object. Ask several consecutive *open-ended questions* to understand your spouse's reasons and viewpoint for selecting that ideal vacation.

In conclusion, always use *open-ended key questions* in order to first *understand* your spouse's inner feelings about an issue before searching for a solution. Without fully comprehending your spouse's viewpoint and reasons for their position, an agreed-upon solution will be difficult.

75. NEVER INTERRUPT YOUR SPOUSE

For almost every troubled marriage, interruptions are a serious problem. *Interruptions may actually be the number-one predictor for unhappiness, separation, or divorce.* When you interrupt each other and use a loud volume, there is no *echoing* and that frequently leads to yelling, which threatens the relationship. Due to interruptions, disappointments and hurts will rarely get resolved, and unresolved issues lead to dissatisfaction and often divorce. Numerous unhappy marital partners have told me, "My spouse has the horrible habit of interrupting me."

At the heart of most *interruptions* is a spouse with impatience and poor listening skills. Another cause is a spouse who only wants to monologue, not dialogue. When a spouse is into monologues, the only way the other partner can express their opinion will be through an interruption.

Think about television talk shows. The interviewer invites two people with differing political perspectives to discuss a topic. Eventually the two participants begin interrupting each other, and they start raising their voices and even disrespecting the other person's viewpoint. For whatever reason, this loud arguing increases viewers, which then increases advertising dollars, and this makes the TV network very happy.

A significant negative result of interruptions is withdrawal and even a refusal to discuss the issues because you fear your opinion will not be heard. To be continually interrupted is frustrating and disheartening for every spouse. Interruptions lead to avoidance of discussing hurts. Withdrawal or avoidance is a significant factor for unhappiness, separation, or divorce.

One of my main goals with this disagreement skills chapter is to help you ABSOLUTELY AVOID INTERRUPTIONS. Establishing guidelines to avoid interruptions is essential for your marital satisfaction. For your marriage and for hopefully all couples reading this book, my prayer is that you utilize the guidelines in this disagreement skills chapter and NEVER INTERRUPT one another.

Say this out loud: *I will always respect what my spouse shares with me by refusing to interrupt!*

76. BE SOLUTION-FOCUSED

The issue is problematic words or behaviors, NOT your spouse's character. Your marriage is always more important than your hurt. There is only a "win" when both of you "win" for your marriage and feel equally good about the *solution*. In order to find *solutions*, both spouses must seek understanding, information, and facts. Without knowledge, solutions are difficult. Proverbs 18:15 states, "The mind of the prudent [always] acquires knowledge, and the ear of the wise [always] seeks knowledge" (AMP).

If a relationship has even one unhealthy spouse, arguments, fights, and conflicts are usually the norm, because that person has deficient thinking. Spouses with deficient thinking actually look for blame and conflict, enjoying the drama. Most significantly, a troubled spouse cannot problem-solve, look for *solutions*, and make necessary "couple corrections" in the marriage.

On the other hand, a healthy spouse is flexible, is adaptable, and can problem-solve one marital concern after another. A wholesome partner is not a fighter, but a negotiator who is constantly looking for *solutions* with the *I need your help* approach. Hence, two healthy spouses have the ability to "couple correct" by finding answers so the relationship is better.

The mantra in the business world is "Do not bring me a problem unless you have a solution." It should be likewise for your marriage: When you ask for an *I need your help* discussion, propose a win-win *solution* in specific behavioral terms that will be in the best interests of both of you. A solution should never lead to a win-lose outcome. Before sharing your hurt, always have *solutions* in your mind and, even better, write them down. Without solutions to the heartache, you are only being a critical complainer.

When you have solutions prepared before you start the discussion, you diminish the temptation for an attack on your spouse's character. *Solutions* focus more on improvement than just assaulting your spouse. *Solutions* also help you be more patient and understanding to avoid a loud and fast argument. Without proposing initial solutions for your heartache, you limit the possibilities for a successful discussion.

When you are giving a solution, ask yourself, "Am I proposing my solution in a loving manner? Is my motive to find a solution so we both feel good about the outcome? Will the solution I am seeking help or hurt our relationship? Do I always have to be right and make the final decision?"

Next, allow your spouse to express their *solutions* for the hurt as well. Perhaps allow your partner to provide not just one but two or three *solutions*. Then, confirm with each other points of agreement with the various options. Perhaps even *echo* what you agree upon before proceeding any further with the discussion. Finally, both of you in one sentence state your understanding of the proposed *solution* for resolving the hurt.

Certainly, you are human, and you do have errors in judgment. So, in your humanness, your solution may not always be the best. Admit at times that your partner may have a good understanding of the problem and perhaps even a better solution. At a minimum, be willing to compromise, and let your primary goal be to demonstrate love toward your spouse through the discussion process of finding a *solution*. Happy couples find win-win answers to their hurts, and they almost never have a winner-loser outcome.

77. TAKE A TIME-OUT

Hopefully, the disagreement guidelines in this chapter will make the need for a *time-out* a rare occurrence. Either of you can stop a disagreement discussion that is starting to get out of control with loud and fast conversation. If the discussion becomes heated, argumentative, or filled with name-calling, you may need to literally give your spouse an athletic *time-out* signal. A *time-out* will allow both of you to relax, calm down, and pray for solutions rather than place blame on each other.

One way to determine that a time-out may be necessary is by using the words *pinch* or *ouch*. I define a *pinch* or *ouch* as a hurtful word, action, or facial expression that causes you to feel devalued or demeaned. A physical pinch or ouch hurts, but it does not bring blood. Likewise, an *emotional pinch* or *ouch* hurts but is not extremely painful.

So, during the discussion, whenever you experience a hurt, you say out loud, "pinch" or "ouch." No one wants to experience a pinch or ouch numerous times, so after a second or third utterance of the word *pinch* or *ouch*, you may want to make the athletic *time-out* signal.

Have a physical separation in which each of you moves to different rooms or perhaps one of you even goes outside for a walk. The partner signaling the time-out will determine the amount of time. I suggest thirty minutes to twenty-four hours. During the time apart, pray for your spouse and your marriage. Ask God to change your heart and give you both patience and understanding to resolve your hurt. Pray for God's guidance in finding a solution and not blame.

Finally, during the *time-out*, I encourage both of you to write down three items. First, define the problem again in just one sentence. Second, write down what you both agree on. Third, provide alternative solutions that were not given prior to the time-out.

Remember, one of your goals is to avoid harsh endings because that is a major reason for separation and divorce. A *time-out* is an excellent tool for diminishing an escalation that could damage your marriage.

78. EVALUATE THE FREQUENCY OF YOUR CONCERNS

How often do you find it necessary to constructively correct, criticize, complain, give unsolicited advice, etc.? In addition, are you always seeking to retaliate for every little occurrence? No matter how well-intentioned your concerns, evaluate how frequently you are criticizing your spouse. Jude 16 speaks to every spouse about a significant negative: "These people are [habitual] murmurers, griping, and complaining" (AMP).

Sometimes you may have no idea just how negative you are being within the relationship. Continual nagging is being a "snouser," sticking your nose too frequently into your spouse's life or continually criticizing aspects of your relationship.

In an objective way, assess just how often you give unsolicited advice, acting like a "snouser," as well as the frequency of your complaints. In addition, log your words and behaviors in a spiral notebook whenever you do any form of the "Cs": *correct, criticize, complain,* or *condemn.* Recording your "Cs" is an objective way to assess if you are being a miserable "snouser." Hopefully, your attitude is not creating constant tension and stress within your relationship.

Insecure or overly sensitive spouses are more fragile and tender, causing them to have numerous concerns. Please also revisit Lesson 5 regarding *scratches, cuts,* and *lacerations.* Very simply, happy spouses have infrequent concerns by only addressing cuts and lacerations. In conclusion, to evaluate the abundancy of your concerns, ask two questions: "How often do I use *I need your help* with my spouse?" And "How often does my spouse say *I need your help?*" Hopefully, the answer to both questions is "rarely."

CHAPTER VII

HABITS THAT SECURE GOD-PLEASING FINANCIAL HARMONY

1 Timothy has two excellent verses on creating marital *financial harmony* and avoiding painful sorrow with marital money. For financial peace we read, "But godliness *actually* is a source of great gain when accompanied by contentment [that contentment which comes from a sense of inner confidence based on the sufficiency of God]" (1 Timothy 6:6 AMP). To help avoid grief and marital misery, God states, "For the love of money [that is, the greedy desire for it and the willingness to gain it unethically] is a root of all sorts of evil, and some by longing for it have wandered away from the faith and pierced themselves [through and through] with many sorrows" (1 Timothy 6:10 AMP), including divorce. This chapter does not include Bible verses with every lesson because the goal is simple marital financial principles.

Monetary boundaries help to effectively construct a satisfying marriage. Unfortunately, a common problem for many unhappy couples is an inability to set up clear guidelines for money management. The number-one thing that couples fight about is money. I estimate that three-fourths of couples argue more about money than time together, sexual intimacy, household tasks, and annoyances.

Healthy financial discussions are very important, and yet this is one of the most difficult topics for most couples. My goal is not to give you a detailed financial plan but simply to help you establish healthy habits for securing financial harmony within your marriage. The lessons from this chapter will allow you to handle money in an orderly way through commonsense guidelines and mutually agreed-upon financial goals. The twelve recommendations in this chapter are generally briefer than the lessons in other chapters because the goal is to provide simple basic financial ground rules for better marital money management.

With the financial knowledge you glean from this chapter, you can now sit down together and make a list of guidelines for managing your own household finances. Instead of money habits producing tension, your fiscal planning will provide an opportunity to increase the love and respect you have for each other in order to build a solid financial foundation.

79. THREE FINANCIAL ABSOLUTES

First Absolute: Be content! Evaluate these statements to determine if this might describe you: "I shop and spend when I am unhappy to fill a void." Or this assertion: "When I get bored, have nothing to do, and have a lot of free time on my hands, I will spend money in an attempt to feel better." Another spouse said, "To build my self-worth, I am always thinking about my next purchase because I believe that *purchasing things* will enhance my self-esteem."

A vacuum in the heart can only be filled by God. Simply put, the love of God is what truly satisfies all your heart's desires.

Money and objects never bring happiness, but having the income you need to pay your monthly bills without borrowing money can relieve a significant amount of personal and marital distress. Thus, be content with a bed, a roof over your head, and perhaps a car to drive. Things are only temporary, but God's love is permanent.

Not being content leads to struggles both for you personally as well as for your marriage. Frequently, the spouse with the higher income is content while the other spouse wants to spend more and more due to a lack of contentment with what they bring financially to the marriage. Please recognize if that is your marital dynamic. One spouse's discontentment can make the other spouse unhappy, while mutual financial contentment makes both of you satisfied. Only seeking God will bring contentment because "things" will never achieve that goal.

Second Absolute: NEVER be a spender! This unquestionable mantra, "NEVER be a spender," is closely tied to the first absolute, because almost 100 percent of the time, when one spouse overspends, marital dissatisfaction is the outcome. If you constantly want to spend and, even worse, overspend, you will never be satisfied—not with life, not with your spouse, and not even with yourself.

A spender will often make excuses with statements like: "I am purchasing items to make our home nicer"; "I am buying clothes for you"; "I am purchasing things for our children or grandchildren." There just seems to always be a justification in order for money to be spent, frequently on a daily basis. A spender simply just spends without any concern for meeting the household budget. A spender also lacks the important attribute of healthy self-denial.

Again, overspending is a symptom of emotional emptiness and constant discontent. If you struggle with continually "wanting more"—a new car, the best new appliances, a new home, new expensive projects, or new expensive "toys"—realize that constantly "wanting more" can damage your marital satisfaction. Perhaps demonstrate goodwill and assess your spending habits by not making any purchases for one month.

Third Absolute: NEVER have financial secrets! Financial secrets involve hiding money, being dishonest about the cost of items, or actually lying about overspending. BOTH of you should know ALL the income, expenses, savings, investments, and credit card expenditures that occur within the marriage. Not having full knowledge of all financial accounts leads to distrust, and distrust leads to dissatisfaction.

80. USE THE THREE "Ds" FOR MAKING PURCHASES

"My spouse never asks, just spends," is a frequent comment made by wives and husbands with a money wedge in their fractured marriage. Overspending spouses often retort, "Why is it such a big deal?" I have found irresponsible or impulsive spending to be one of the major sources for marital discord. Hasty, impulsive purchases create debt, debt increases frustration, frustration produces resentment, and resentment generates hostility.

Making significant purchases requires understanding and patience. Your money decisions are not simply about spending, but they are about fostering habits that lead to a lifetime of financial peace.

Proverbs 21:5 reads, "The plans of the diligent lead to profit as surely as haste leads to poverty" (NIV). Your money should be handled in an orderly way so that good stewardship is practiced. Smart couples discuss money matters in order to give their relationship a better chance of being successful. When it comes to household money, communication lines need to be wide open.

Your spending of money is not nearly as important as the way you practice the *three "Ds"*: **disclose, discuss**, and **decide** how to spend money. A common practice in business and government requires approval for certain purchases; it should be likewise for your successful marriage. I am not recommending that you must disclose all purchases to one another, only those items that you consider discretionary. Jointly managing your important major purchases is unequivocally an essential habit.

You will first need to discuss how you define discretionary and nondiscretionary spending. Or I often ask couples to agree that any single item above a set amount would be considered discretionary. An *approval limit* is discussed in the next lesson.

Once you have agreement on the definition of discretionary spending, if an item is above that *approval limit*, utilize the *three "Ds"—disclose, discuss*, and *decide*. **Disclose** to your spouse when you would like to buy clothing, household items, leisure products, etc., that exceed the set amount. **Discuss** together the pros and cons of such a purchase. Finally, **decide** together if the item is a need or a want and whether it is within the budget. A major purchase should never be made without the *three "Ds,"* because financial agreement keeps you connected. One spouse said, "The *three 'Ds'* saved our marriage because the *three 'Ds'* finally made us accountable to one another and our frivolous spending came to a halt."

For *financial harmony*, it's important to have a game plan for purchases. Managing important financial decisions provides an opportunity to love each other. When both of you agree to the same purchasing guidelines, you have a recipe for financial peace. So always **disclose, discuss**, **and** **decide** together!

81. HAVE AN APPROVAL LIMIT

High-priced purchases are usually discretionary rather than non-discretionary. Without a spending *approval limit* on discretionary items, damage can easily be done to your marriage. However, having a financial agreement threshold reduces stress for both of you.

I counseled a financially comfortable couple with significant money issues. The main problem was—no *approval limit* guideline. One example, the husband purchased an apartment building and said he "forgot to mention" to his wife he was thinking about that major purchase. Eventually, both agreed upon an approval limit of $500.

I define an *approval limit* as a set amount, above which neither one of you independently can make a purchase. From the couples I have counseled, the range for that set amount has varied from $10 all the way up to $500. Having that set amount will cut down on overspending, thus reducing marital conflict.

Although most grocery items are nondiscretionary, rarely is there a problem with groceries, since few products exceed the approval limit price. However, I have observed some marital strain when a spouse purchases expensive specialty items like lobster, filet mignon, or even organic items that can be double the price of regular items, thus exceeding the approval limit. You may need to set an approval limit for certain grocery purchases to diminish tension.

There are many benefits associated with an *approval limit*. First, with major purchases, you will make mutual decisions that help ensure you stay within the budget. Second, you usually improve your credit because you avoid high debt. Third, spending boundaries diminish your stress both personally and financially because your spending is more predictable. Fourth, spending limits will automatically provide more insight into the importance of a monthly budget. Fifth, frequent shopping is often diminished because purchases are not immediately possible if those expenditures exceed the approval limit.

I have found that most happy couples have some type of an *approval limit* to reduce the tension of overspending. Be exceedingly wise and have an approval limit above which a discretionary purchase cannot be made without implementing the *three "Ds"*.

82. RECORD EVERY EXPENDITURE

Marital satisfaction is enhanced when both spouses know where all the money is going as well as the why. One way for both of you to obtain a sharper grasp of this is to record daily every expenditure, no matter how small the amount, for one month. I also encourage you to do this exercise twice per year to improve your money management.

Perhaps place a spiral notebook either on your kitchen counter or bedroom dresser as a daily reminder. Again, make sure you include ALL expenses. So even if you only spend fifty cents at the gas station for a candy bar, record that in your notebook. Some couples also place receipts in a jar to keep track of expenses.

Frequently, you may discover unhealthy spending patterns that may financially damage your marriage. One spouse was shocked to find that she stopped at the grocery store daily and purchased "junk" items that caused her family to have weight issues. Another couple mentally estimated that they spent $350 per month on fast food for supper on the way home from their children's activities. After one month of recording every purchase, they were shocked to discover the actual amount was over $850.

For financial harmony, during one month at least once per year, will you please *record daily every expenditure?*

83. "TAKE 3" FOR MAJOR PURCHASES

One of the significant sources for relationship dissatisfaction is impulsive spending. Spontaneous purchases usually also exceed the *approval limit* (Lesson 81). Unfortunately, too many spouses have an immediate "see it, want it, get it" mentality, and that has been the downfall of many marriages. Hasty purchases create debt, debt increases frustration, frustration produces resentment, and resentment often generates arguments.

Relationships benefit from two spouses who have patience and adhere to financial guidelines with discretionary purchases. Learning to delay spending can create a lifetime habit that will lead to *marital financial harmony*. When two spouses are able to overcome a "spend now" philosophy, both are often more relaxed, creating a more gratifying marriage.

Thus, I intentionally made this a separate guideline because immediate gratification threatens your budget and relationship contentment. Furthermore, too many couples hurriedly apply the *three "Ds"* to major purchases, agree that the criteria were met, and then actually spend above their budget.

GO SLOW when you have a major purchase. Thus, *"take 3"* may translate into three days, three weeks, or even three months. For example, a newer car or a different home may be a three-month discussion before finally deciding upon your purchase.

In addition, *"take 3"* may also mean involving three family members or friends that have a particular expertise with your major purchase. Have them write down their pros and cons and then give you their list. Involving family and friends can be beneficial, but it also can create significant problems, so be careful when asking for their advice. Also, DO NOT include family members and friends in your discussions together; that is just between the two of you. The friends and family pros and cons list is only to assist your discussion.

Your marriage will only improve and grow through implementation of the *"take 3"* guideline. By putting *"take 3"* among your important financial guidelines, you increase the probabilities for overcoming a major heartache that harms 75 percent of couples.

84. JOINT CHECKING

Smart couples are joined at the hip when talking about money. Being financially unified usually means having a *joint checking* account. Most wise couples have one joint checking account in order to be on the same page with the marital finances. "Joint" implies that you are not only one flesh in God's eyes but also have "oneness" in the all-important financial area. If you do have three accounts: his account, her account, and a joint account, both of you need to be fully aware of the balances for all three accounts.

Please let me explain why separate accounts create several negatives. First, you may unintentionally view your marriage as a business partnership rather than a "one flesh union." Separate accounts may also lead to the attitude of "your" money versus "my" money rather than "OUR" money. Finally, with a separate account, if either one of you has impulsive spending habits or a compulsivity to purchase very regularly, there is a greater temptation to avoid the *three "Ds"* or *approval limit*.

If one of you believes you must have separate accounts, then split up the household bills. Each of you can then pay a percentage of your marital expenses based upon your income. For example, if your two incomes are $25,000 and $50,000, the percentages would be 33% and 67%. A fair distribution will usually produce a richer relationship.

Having a *joint account* is the least complicated way to handle finances. When you have a joint account, you are also much more likely to discuss spending, budgeting, and financial goals. If you struggle agreeing upon a *joint checking account*, try a pros and cons list to hopefully recognize the benefits.

85. BUDGET WITH A PERCENT SPENDING PLAN

The foundation for marital financial peace is contentment and discipline. Certainly, find your contentment in God and trust in Him. However, that does not mean you should avoid a budget and a percent spending plan. A *budget* actually forces you to discipline your spending, and that results in service to God with your money. Having respectful budget discussions actually strengthens your relationship because you are establishing mutual financial goals that are extremely important for a solid marital foundation.

Financial planning needs to be an ongoing conversation. Ideally, it is best to discuss these things when you are not in the midst of a financial crisis or have a major decision to make. Thus, always discuss when things are going well. Work for open financial communication to achieve your budgeting goals. If necessary, find a financial mentor who can teach you what to do and what not to do with your money goals.

I suggest you go online and find a basic budget form. Independently, each of you will complete the budget form. Just separately researching all of your expenses will be beneficial in itself for your marriage. After you are both finished, compare your budgets and mutually decide upon a marital budget. Then have monthly money meetings, or at a minimum, twice per year revisit your marital budget.

Next, independently write down what you think are appropriate percentages for major expense categories. Consider the following areas:

1. offerings to God
2. housing
3. automobiles
4. insurance
5. food
6. clothing
7. entertainment and travel
8. eating out
9. medical
10. savings/investments
11. debt retirement
12. miscellaneous

This is not an exhaustive list, but hopefully it can guide your percent spending discussions. For example, you might agree to spend 25 percent or less on housing, no more than 5 percent on auto loans, 15 percent or less on food, no more than 15 percent on entertainment and travel, etc. Of course, the total should equal 100 percent.

The positive goal is to have a mutually agreed-upon budget that also takes into account your *percent spending plan*. Definitely, having mutually agreed-upon specific financial goals will diminish disagreements and enhance your marital satisfaction.

86. KEEP A RESERVE FUND FOR SIX MONTHS OF EXPENSES

Nearly 80 percent of people live from paycheck to paycheck, which can be extremely stressful. A six-month reserve fund is an essential financial goal. Hopefully it will never happen, but if both of you were to lose your jobs, you need to have sufficient savings to cover ALL your expenses for six months.

To accomplish that goal, eliminate all spending that isn't unequivocally essential. By essential, I mean medical expenses, recurring bills for the home or cars, grocery expenses, and any other crucial expenditures. This process will force you to give up gourmet coffee, going out to eat except for *date your mate*, clothing purchases, movies, etc. Basically, you are only making payments for the absolute necessities of life. Living a life without indulgences can be a great exercise in self-discipline.

This method will help achieve the goal of being debt-free. I define debt-free as only having a mortgage and car payment. With a six-month reserve fund, your relationship will be more gratifying, allowing you to implement all the habits that will enhance your oneness.

87. SAVE 10 PERCENT OF YOUR NET INCOME

Always live within your means! After you have a six-month reserve fund in place, your next goal is to not spend more than 90
percent of your net income. Budget what you spend so you can
save a percentage of your net income at the end of every month.
This percentage is an investment in your future. Hopefully, the
10 percent savings is in addition to your retirement monies. DO
NOT use this 10 percent for future entertainment, hobbies, travel, luxury home projects, etc. This 10 percent is intended to build
a second fund for *significant future purchases or emergencies.*

For many couples, 10 percent is an unrealistic goal. If that is
your situation, perhaps start at 1 percent of your net income,
and when you are financially able, increase to 2 percent, then
3 percent, etc. Whatever your percentage, downsize your lifestyle and commit to spend less than you earn each month. This
is another short lesson, but I hope you are starting to **develop a
saving mentality!**

88. CASH OR CONVENIENCE CREDIT CARDS

Credit cards are good, but credit card debt is really, really bad!
Credit cards have wonderful positive benefits, but they can also
have a negative financial impact when the balance is not paid in
FULL at the end of each month. Both of you must understand
that credit cards are *cash* or *convenience cards.*

Due to a lack of self-discipline or compulsive buying disorder,
for many couples, credit cards are a huge NO-NO! Again, both of
you must recognize that all credit card balances must be **paid in
FULL at the end of the month**. To achieve that goal, you must
be very self-disciplined and avoid even a small balance on *every
credit card.*

If for whatever reason you are unable to pay the entire credit
card balance at the end of every month, then DO NOT use credit

cards. Due to unpaid balances, many marriages have been deeply fractured by high interest payments that eventually break the marriage budget and may even lead to bankruptcy.

On the positive side, besides convenience, *credit cards* have several substantial advantages or perks. At the end of the year, some credit card companies will break down your yearly expenditures for evaluation purposes. In addition, based upon reward points, some credit card companies provide frequent flier miles, gift cards, and even credit to your account.

Finally, to avoid spending temptation, limit your number of credit cards. Based upon the rewards that you are seeking, perhaps have a maximum of three or four credit cards. Bottom line: When you have enough discipline to pay off your balance every month, *credit cards* have wonderful benefits. Per Lesson 87, your goal is to spend less than you make so credit card debt should never be a problem.

89. HAVE YOUR OWN DISCRETIONARY MONEY

Many marriages benefit from both spouses having pocket money or "fun money" every week. So set aside a certain amount of money every week for each of you. A spousal "fun fund" can destress your relationship and help create a relaxed environment for both of you.

One benefit is that you won't feel deprived or guilty when you self-indulge. Neither one of you will feel the need to be a "money monitor," tracking each penny spent. Bottom line: Each of you will feel less controlled by your partner.

This pocket money is not for gas, groceries, or any other budgeted item. Simply, this is money that you do not have to give an account for at the end of the week. Sometimes this "play money" inspires creativity. Use pocket money for a lunch out, a personal treat, or perhaps saving toward a special gift for your spouse, etc.

Definitely include this *discretionary* amount in your budget under "miscellaneous expenses." Depending on a couple's income, this play money amount will generally range from $5 to $100 per week. When thinking about this *discretionary money,* please remember Lesson 87 and the goal of saving 10 percent of your net income.

90. GOD AND CHARITABLE CONTRIBUTIONS

I am not going to give a sermon on *offerings to God and charities.* Nonetheless, whenever you give some type of offering, your money is not given to a church or charitable organization; your money is really being given to almighty God who, through Jesus Christ's death and resurrection, has bestowed His grace and given the gift of eternal life in heaven.

There are some wonderful Bible verses on stewardship and giving back to almighty God. Psalm 24:1 states, "The earth is the Lord's, and everything in it, the world, and all who live in it" (NIV). Proverbs 3:9 declares, "Honor the Lord with your wealth, with the firstfruits of all your crops" (NIV). Finally, here is the most well-known passage on giving: "Let each one give [thoughtfully and with purpose] just as he has decided in his heart, not grudgingly or under compulsion, for God loves a cheerful giver [and delights in the one whose heart is in his gift]" (2 Corinthians 9:7 AMP).

So being a wise steward is absolutely essential. God is glorified, and good stewardship is practiced when couples give first to the Lord and then handle all other living expenses. Our goal is to serve almighty God with our money—both with offerings to the Lord and gifts to charitable organizations. Our heavenly Father wants us to wisely use our money.

External giving is an indication of the internal condition of your heart. A genuine heart for God almost always has a heart for others, including one's spouse. A couple united in gratitude to God for His bountiful goodness and an eternal home, will also not be too busy for each other because they avoid focusing on the mundane things of this temporary world. In fact, exercising good stewardship together will actually build intimacy and strengthen your emotional bond. Most importantly, growing closer to God creates a special oneness, and that often happens through giving to God as a couple.

Finally, our *offerings to God* reflect whether God is our master or money is our master (see Matthew 6:24). Our offerings to God are truly a reflection of our Christ-centered heart. Thus, give together to the Lord with a cheerful heart and keep your eyes on the eternal mansion awaiting all believers!

CONCLUSION

You now possess the skills, tools, and practical answers for achieving a happy relationship! Please do not use any lessons as a "weapon" against your spouse by saying, "Look at that lesson, I told you so." Simply discuss in a loving manner those essential skills or behaviors that have been missing. Sometimes the difference between marital satisfaction and a devastating divorce is the *implementation of just one Simple Habit!*

Always remember, a gratifying marriage is a *labor of love* that requires *hard work* by both of you. Determination plus effort is what it takes to form beneficial nurturing behaviors that will eventually become regular habits. At times, you may be able to implement behavior changes immediately and quickly see the benefits. However, most of the time, replacing your various unhealthy habits with positive new ones may take weeks, or months, or years. But it can be done.

At first, employing your new behaviors may not seem necessarily satisfying, but you can rejoice that your new habits will create marital satisfaction. And the more healthy habits you possess as a couple, the higher probability you will develop a loving relationship.

So, do everything possible to improve as a spouse because your constructive changes enhance the probabilities for a rewarding relationship. Changing any unhealthy life habit is difficult, so be patient with yourself and your spouse when improvement is necessary for marital happiness. As stated other times in the book, *become comfortable being uncomfortable* as you improve and grow as a spouse.

Thankfully, minor behavioral adjustments, yes even one simple new behavior, can lead to much greater satisfaction in your relationship. Practice, practice, practice with your new healthy behaviors until those *new healthy habits* are formed! Understand that when you develop healthy meaningful habits, you are saying to your spouse, "I care about you and our happiness together!"

Initially, I encourage each of you to identify one unhealthy habit that is diminishing your marital satisfaction the most. Realize that you may choose different habits for improvement. Daily, focus on changing those two significant troubling behaviors into new positive habits. Repetition is the mother of all learning, so repeat over and over the new healthy behaviors until you form beneficial habits. Next, each of you choose another practical habit you want to focus on, then each of you select a third *Simple Habit*, etc.

A satisfying relationship is your destination, but understand that attaining an enjoyable marriage is a lifelong journey of *good, dependable daily effort*. One happy spouse said, *"Consistency and discipline* in using the *Simple Habits* has diminished our marital tension and increased our satisfaction. Many *Simple Habits* filled in the potholes and now our marriage highway is a much smoother road."

So please never leave your marital satisfaction to luck or chance. *Diligently plan* to have a happy, satisfying marriage! One absolutely essential question for both of you to answer is: "How much *time* and *effort* will I devote to implementing the *Simple Habits* each day?" Every six months, and at a minimum once per year, *read aloud together one or two lessons per day* from *Simple Habits for Marital Happiness*.

By reading and rereading the book, along with thoroughly discussing these skills and tools, your dream for a satisfying marriage can now come true. As you incorporate these proven ideas and practical answers, you will feel better about yourself as a spouse and have more confidence in developing a successful gratifying marriage. Through your daily efforts, these *Simple Habits for Marital Happiness* will eventually result in consistent marital satisfaction.

May our almighty God richly bless your hard work in improving as a spouse and growing together in order to build a strong, loving marriage!

ABOUT THE AUTHOR

Randall Schroeder, PhD, earned a Bachelor of Science from Concordia University Chicago, and received a Master's of Education in Administration from Wayne State University in Detroit, Michigan. He also earned a Master of Divinity from Concordia Theological Seminary in Fort Wayne, Indiana and holds a Ph.D. in Marriage and Family Therapy from The Chicago Theological Seminary.

Dr. Schroeder is a retired professor of pastoral counseling at Concordia Theological Seminary in Fort Wayne, Indiana. For nearly 25 years he taught a number of classes in marriage counseling, premarital counseling, family counseling, crisis counseling, and more.

Dr. Schroeder has a successful counseling practice and is passionate about helping individuals, couples, and families enjoy satisfying personal lives and relationships. Within Christian circles, he is a well-known relationship speaker. A very popular presenter, audiences enjoy his influential style of encouraging and guiding individuals, couples, parents, and relationships to succeed.

Randy and his wife, Ginny, have been happily married for over forty years and have two married sons, along with six grandchildren.

Please find additional practical wisdom on marriage, parenting, and life at www.DrRandySchroeder.com.